Smoothie Splash!

Smoothie
Splash!

150 fast,
fruity &
fabulous recipes

by Holly Jennings

Main Street
A division of Sterling Publishing Co., Inc.
New York

Library of Congress Cataloging-in-Publication Data Available

10 9 8 7 6 5 4 3 2 1

Published by Sterling Publishing Co., Inc.
387 Park Avenue South, New York, NY 10016

© 2005 by Holly Jennings
Photographs © 2005 by Theresa Raffetto

Distributed in Canada by Sterling Publishing
c/o Canadian Manda Group, 165 Dufferin Street
Toronto, Ontario, Canada M6K 3H6

Distributed in Great Britain by
Chrysalis Books Group PLC
The Chrysalis Building, Bramley Road,
London W10 6SP, England

Distributed in Australia by Capricorn Link
(Australia) Pty. Ltd.
P.O. Box 704, Windsor, NSW 2756, Australia

Design by Liz Trovato
Photographs by Theresa Raffetto
Food Stylist: William Smith
Prop Stylist: Barb Fritz

Printed in China

Sterling ISBN 1-4027-2934-0

For information about custom editions,
special sales, premium and corporate purchases,
please contact Sterling Special Sales
Department at 800-805-5489 or
specialsales@sterlingpub.com.

Intro

duction

Smoothies—they're simply all the rage. They overflow with delicious taste and nutritious ingredients, and they have a winning texture—thick, creamy, and frosty. In addition, smoothies are perfect for any time of day or night—from a breakfast eye-opener to a midday energy boost to an after-dinner nightcap. And the best part? Top-drawer smoothies are a cinch to make, with only a minimum amount of advance preparation.

Great taste, good nutrition, and easy prep are my criteria for great smoothies, and what has guided the making of the recipes in this book. So please, rev up your blender and come explore the world of smoothies with me.

Smoothie Philosophy 101

Use local organic produce whenever possible. When produce is in season, always try to buy from local organic farmers—whether at a farm stand, farmers' market, or natural foods store that sells local produce. Your smoothies will taste better and be better for you.

Use frozen fruit and frozen liquid ingredients (juice, tea, etc.) Frozen ingredients work on several levels: They serve as a flavor base, create a thick texture, and contribute to the desired ice-cold temperature—all without diluting flavor or nutritional value. You can buy frozen unsweetened organic fruit or freeze your own. Note: Standard ice cube trays were used to make frozen cubes in the recipes. One cube is the equivalent of two tablespoons of liquid.

Don't use ice cubes. It's tempting to use ice cubes because they contribute a chilly temperature and thick texture to smoothies. But they're entirely lacking in two important qualities—flavor and nutrition. But, never say never: If your goal is to make a low-calorie smoothie, ice cubes will add volume and thickness without calories. A handful of the smoothies in Chapter Two—called "Crushes"—were made with this in mind.

Avoid products with refined sugar or artificial sweeteners, such as frozen yogurt and sorbet. (Unless, that is, you're purposely setting out to make a sweet, dessert-like smoothie and extra calories aren't an issue.) This is one of the most basic points of my smoothie philosophy. If you've been to a smoothie bar, you know that frozen yogurt or sorbet is often used as a base in smoothies. I consider these to be nothing more than milk-shakes in disguise. Instead, sweeten your smoothies with the natural sugars in fruit, other natural sweeteners (such as honey), or, if you're trying to cut calories, stevia, a natural alternative to artificial sweeteners.

For the best smoothie experience, drink them soon after they're made. The ingredients in smoothies tend to separate if they're allowed to sit. In addition, the nutritional content of fruit and especially fresh juices diminishes quickly.

Smoothie-Making Tips

- For the coldest smoothie possible, use everything chilled or, when recommended, frozen.

- If you have the patience, allow deep-frozen fruit to sit out at room temperature for about 20 minutes.

- If a recipe calls for frozen cubes, break these up in your blender first, using the pulse button. If your blender is not powerful enough to break up frozen cubes, you may want to break up the cubes manually: Put cubes in a freezer bag and bang away at them with the bottom of a small pan.

- Follow the frozen cubes with liquids, then yogurt or silken tofu, then fruits and vegetables. Finally, nuts, seeds, or other supplements should be added last and while the blender is running.

- Start on low speed, and gradually increase it.

Freezing Fruit

Specific directions for preparing different fruits for freezing can be found in the fruit profiles that follow; however, some basic steps are worth mentioning here. Rinse and dry all fruit thoroughly (except for strawberries, raspberries, and blackberries, which should never be rinsed unless they're noticeably dirty or have been sprayed with pesticides). Peel skins if necessary, or as to your preference. I recommend peeling peaches and apples. Nectarine and plum skins, by contrast, are more delicate. All seeds or stones should be removed, and fruit should be cut into half-inch pieces for the blender. I don't recommend freezing kiwifruit, melons, or pears, because their delicate flavor and texture don't hold up.

Place prepared pieces of fruit or berries in a large freezer bag, squeeze out as much air as possible, and place on a flat shelf in the freezer. If an empty freezer shelf is not available, freeze fruit in a single layer on a cookie sheet for at least 30 minutes, then transfer to a freezer bag. Label and date the bag. Try to use frozen fruit within two weeks of freezing, although it can keep for much longer—generally up to six months.

Portions

Most of the recipes in this book make 16 ounces, yielding one large smoothie or two average-sized servings. The exceptions are the smoothies in Chapter Seven and some of the frozen yogurt/ice cream–based smoothies in Chapter Six, each of which yield 10 to 12 ounces.

Smoothie Ingredients

Binders

Most of the smoothies in this book are made with a base of milk (almond, dairy, oat, rice, or soy), yogurt, and/or silken tofu. They bind the ingredients together in a creamy base and help balance the sugar content of fruit. To pump up the nutritional value, be sure to use milks that are enriched.

Almond Milk. A blend of crushed almonds and water, almond milk has a subtly nutty, slightly sweet flavor.

Dairy Milk. Most noted for its calcium, protein, and vitamin D, milk is also a source of phosphorus, potassium, and vitamins A and B. Use low-fat or nonfat milk if you're watching saturated fat.

Oat Milk. Made from oat groats (hulled grain broken into fragments), oat bran, and water, oat milk has a mild oat flavor with a touch of sweetness. With the highest amount of carbohydrates of any milk, oat milk is great for breakfast and workout smoothies.

Rice Milk. With its creamy appearance and slightly sweet flavor—more neutral than almond or oat milk—rice milk is a great, low-fat alternative to dairy milk.

Soy Milk. A blend of ground cooked soybeans and water, soy milk is a good source of protein, B vitamins, and iron. However, the real cachet of soy milk—and all soy products—is its high levels of isoflavones, which have numerous health benefits. I recommend using full-fat soy milk in smoothies, for

The Blender

Smoothies require only one piece of equipment— a blender, and the sturdier the better. An ordinary household blender will do, but if you're in the market for a new blender, look for one with a powerful motor— 330 watts or higher. It will do the best job of pulverizing ice cubes and fibrous fruit and vegetables and have greater longevity. Food processors also will do the job, though they will not create the same smooth consistency as blenders.

two reasons: Though high in fat, it is low in saturated fat and is cholesterol-free. In addition, it has beneficial essential fatty acids and helps keep hunger at bay. Although some people find soy milk unappealing, when blended with other ingredients in a smoothie, its flavor is undetectable.

Plain Yogurt. This delicious binder, which also adds thickness to a smoothie, is rich in protein, calcium, magnesium, zinc, and riboflavin. Yogurt's bonus is its live bacteria cultures, which boost the immune system and aid digestion. Yogurt is available in full-fat, low-fat, and nonfat forms. To shave a few calories, I use low-fat yogurt in the recipes here, but the choice is yours. Be sure to select yogurt with live cultures (this will be stated on the label). Note that frozen yogurt, along with having abundant refined sugar, does not have the benefit of live cultures.

Silken Tofu. This very soft tofu imparts a thick, silken quality to smoothies. Tofu has the same nutritional and health benefits of soy milk, including high levels of protein, B vitamins, iron, and isoflavones. Silken tofu can be found in the refrigerated or dry-goods section of the grocery store. Note that silken tofu is thicker than yogurt, so if you're using it as a substitute for yogurt, you should use a little less.

Natural Sweeteners

Concentrated Fruit Juices (Unsweetened). Concentrated juices, available at natural food or gourmet grocers, add an extra kick of sweetness and impart fruit-flavored character to smoothies. To make concentrated juice at home, use 1 part organic juice concentrate and 1 1/2 parts water. Since these juices are very high in sugar, use in small amounts, generally 1 to 2 tablespoons.

Honey. Humankind's oldest sweetener, honey, is in a class of its own, with an appealing flavor and numerous medicinal properties, such as helping alleviate allergies and ulcers and healing wounds.

Maple Syrup. This American favorite is as delicious as it is nutritious. Especially rich in calcium, it is also a source of potassium, manganese, magnesium, phosphorus, and iron. Maple syrup has a tendency to mask other ingredients in a smoothie if used in too great a quantity, so start by adding it in small increments.

Stevia. This miracle sweetener, made from the herb stevia, is available at natural food and nutrition stores. Stevia is 400 times sweeter than sugar, yet it contributes zero calories and none of the health consequences that come from eating refined sugar. It is safe for diabetics and those with hypoglycemia, and is ideal for those trying to cut down on their calorie intake.

Fruits

Apples. With 7,500 varieties of apples grown throughout the world, we could eat a different apple each day to keep the doctor away for more than 20 years. But most of us will have to settle for the mere 100 varieties grown in the U.S. Does this ancient fruit warrant its old health adage? Apples have some vitamin C and are rich in potassium and pectin. More than anything, the old "apple a day" saying may come from their ability to help keep us "regular": Pectin decreases the severity of diarrhea, while the sorbitol content acts as a laxative.

Selection: Choose apples that are firm to the touch and have a fresh aroma; they should not smell musty or fermented. They should be heavy for their size and their skins should be bright.

Preparation: Peel if desired, cut in half, remove the core, and cut into half-inch pieces.

Apricots. Apricots are a powerhouse of beta carotene, potassium, and fiber. Take advantage of the delicate flavor of fresh apricots when in season in the summer, and at other times of year use juice and dried apricots.

Selection: Apricots do not improve in flavor after they've been picked, so be careful to avoid hard or pale fruit. They should be plump, slightly soft to the touch, and fragrant.

Preparation: Cut in half, remove the pit, and cut into half-inch pieces.

Bananas. Naturally sweet and creamy, bananas do the best job of creating a faux milkshake experience—without the calories and sugar found in ice cream or frozen yogurt. Bananas are rich in potassium, magnesium, folic acid, and vitamin B_6, and a powerhouse of carbohydrates.

Selection: Since bananas continue to ripen after they've been picked, buy them green, when they're less susceptible to bruising, and let them ripen to your preferred level. Avoid bananas with moldy stems, split skins, or dark areas showing through the skin.

Preparation: Cut bananas into quarters before freezing them, as pieces will be small enough for your blender to handle.

Blackberries. We enjoy plump and juicy blackberries for their taste and the beautiful deep-purple color they add to smoothies. Blackberries are also packed with nutrients: vitamin E, folic acid, vitamin C, and antioxidants.

Selection: Look for whole, plump, dark berries. Avoid berries with the green hulls still attached or those whose color tends toward red. Examine closely for mold at the stem end.

Preparation: Refrigerate in a single layer on a shallow paper towel-lined tray. Never wash blackberries unless they are very dusty, and then only with a quick cold rinse just before using.

Blueberries. This small berry has the highest known antioxidant level of any fruit. Blueberries are also a good source of salicylate, a natural aspirinlike compound that has been shown to reduce inflammation.

Selection: Look for firm blueberries with smooth skins; avoid hard and shriveled berries.

Preparation: Rinse and sort out any berries that are past their prime; remove any stems. Refrigerate for up to a week on a shallow, paper towel-lined tray.

Cantaloupe. Like all melons, cantaloupes have high levels of vitamin C. They are also rich in potassium, vitamin A, folic acid, and, like all orange-fleshed fruits, beta carotene.

Selection: Cantaloupes ripen only a little after they've been picked, so don't buy ones that are quite hard. Look for thick, coarse netting that stands out on the surface and a pale yellow or yellowish-buff color. The stem end should yield slightly to gentle pressure and emit a pleasant odor.

Preparation: Store at room temperature and chill only just before using. Slice off both ends of the cantaloupe. Cut the rind from the melon in thick slices, working from the top to the bottom. Cut the melon in half, remove the seeds, and cut the flesh into half-inch pieces.

Cherries. A good source of vitamins A and C, potassium, magnesium, and phosphorus, cherries also contain anthocyanin, a natural antioxidant which, together with vitamin C, supports the growth of collagen—making cherries good for women at risk of osteoporosis and people who work out regularly.

Selection: Look for bright, plump cherries. Bypass any that are soft, moldy, or bruised. The stems should be green and bendable, not brown and dry.

Preparation: Rinse, remove their stems, and dry on a paper towel-lined tray. Remove pits with a cherry pitter or cut the cherry in half lengthwise, cutting around the pit, and pull the halves away.

Dates, Dried. Not only does the sweet, rich flavor of dried dates make any smoothie more luxurious, the ancient fruit also adds a stash of fiber, potassium, phosphorus, iron, calcium, magnesium, vitamin A, and folic acid.

Selection: Look for dried dates that are plump and have shiny, bright skin.

Preparation: To pit a date, simply cut it in half lengthwise, cutting around the pit, and pull the halves away from the pit. If your dates are not soft and moist, soak them in hot water for 15 minutes.

Figs. Despite their long history, many Americans' experience of figs is sadly limited to Fig Newtons. Though the enjoyment of this cookie has its place, it cannot compare with the flavor of fresh figs in a smoothie. Figs have loads of iron, potassium, and fiber, and are an excellent source of calcium.

Selection: Figs do not travel well, so unless you live in an area where figs are grown, you will be buying figs that have been picked green. However, figs will ripen and improve in flavor if kept at room temperature for a day or two. Place on a shallow paper towel-lined tray in a single layer. Ripe figs are slightly soft to the touch and may have minute breaks in the skin.

Preparation: Rinse with cool water and cut off the tough end of the stem; peel the skin if it seems especially tough. Dried figs should be soaked in hot water for 15 minutes to soften.

Grapefruit. It's easy to understand why this plentiful citrus is a staple at the breakfast table. In addition to providing us with a tart wake-up call, grapefruit is rich in vitamin C, potassium, and pectin, a soluble fiber that can reduce cholesterol levels. For the best taste and maximum nutrients, always use fresh-squeezed, strained grapefruit juice.

Selection: Look for smooth fruit with glossy skin and a sweet smell. Grapefruits should be slightly springy and flat at both ends, and feel heavy for their size.

Preparation: Although recipes in this book use only grapefruit juice, seeded sections can also go into the blender: Hold a peeled grapefruit over a bowl and cut on both sides of the membranes that separate segments; the segments will release from the membranes.

Grapes (White and Red). These little morsels, which add an explosion of delicious flavor to smoothies, go way back. One of the earliest records of grape-growing appeared in an Egyptian wall painting from around 2440 B.C. Grapes are a good source of vitamin C, potassium, and manganese, and are renowned for their restorative powers. Note that red grapes are richer in antioxidants than white.

Selection: Look for seedless grapes that are plump and have saturated color. The sweetest, full-flavored white grapes will be tinged with an amber color.

Preparation: Grapes should be thoroughly rinsed in cold water. Remove grapes from stems and add to smoothies chilled, or, for a thicker, frostier smoothie, frozen.

Honeydew Melon. This sweet melon with pretty pale-green flesh is a good source of vitamin B_6, folic acid, potassium, and particularly vitamin C.

Selection: Honeydews should have a very smooth white rind, sometimes spattered with yellow. When ripe, they are slightly soft to the touch at the blossom end.

Preparation: Store at room temperature and chill only just before using. Cut in quarters, seed the slices, and cut the flesh from the skin.

Kiwifruit. The kiwifruit's emerald green, fragrant flesh is as beautiful as its exterior is plain. Kiwifruit contains almost twice as much vitamin C as an orange, and they're a good source of potassium and fiber.

Selection: Look for plump kiwifruit with no broken skin or dark areas. When ripe, the fruit should give slightly to gentle pressure. It is okay to buy firm fruit at the market, since kiwifruit do ripen after being picked.

Preparation: Cut fruit in half crosswise and scoop out the flesh.

Lemon Juice. A touch of vitamin C-packed lemon juice can be that little something that tweaks a smoothie, transforming it from good to amazing. A teaspoon or two will brighten smoothies, and balance too-sweet flavors. Always used freshly squeezed, strained lemon juice: It tastes better and has more nutrients than store-bought juice.

Selection: Buy lemons that are heavy for their size, have a thin, smooth rind, and are fully yellow in color. Lemons that have a greenish tint won't be as sweet and flavorful.

Preparation: If lemon zest is needed, remember to grate the peel before juicing. Roll a room-temperature lemon back and forth with the palm of your hand to soften it slightly and create more juice; then cut in half and squeeze.

Lime Juice. The juice from this green citrus gem can be used in much same way as lemon juice in a smoothie—to boost flavor or balance sweetness. Lime juice is rich in bioflavonoids and has powerful antibacterial properties. But the most important nutritional value of limes is their high level of vitamin C. In fact, limes are cited in medical history as helping prevent scurvy when the British navy required ships destined for long journeys to take along limes for the crew—thus the nickname limeys for British sailors.

Selection: Like lemons, limes should be heavy for their size. They should be firm and have glossy skin. Steer clear of hard, shrunken limes as well as soft, spongy ones.

Preparation: Follow instructions for lemons.

Mangoes. The heady, unmistakable taste and smooth meaty texture of mangoes lend delicious flavor and creaminess to smoothies. The deep orange color is a dead giveaway to the fruit's high level of beta carotene, but mangoes are also a good source of potassium, vitamin C, and some vitamin B_6 and vitamin E. They also contain the antioxidant beta cryptoxanthin, which may help prevent some types of cervical cancer.

Selection: A ripe mango should be firm but give a little when gently pressed, and should emit a sweet smell. Do not buy mangoes that are soft or have shriveled skin.

Preparation: Mangoes have a large, flat stone that clings to the flesh and must be cut away. Stand the mango on its stem end with a narrow side toward you and cut the flesh away from the pit. Avoid the fibrous flesh near the pit's surface.

Nectarines. Smooth-skinned, sweet-tasting nectarines (a variety of peach) are a good source of vitamin C and are even richer in antioxidants than other peaches.

Selection: Look for nectarines that are firm—but not hard—and plump. The background color should never be green, which indicates they were picked too early.

Preparation: Nectarine skin tends to be very delicate, so peeling is usually not necessary. To remove the pit, cut the nectarine all the way around along the seam. If the nectarine is a freestone variety, you will be able to separate the halves by gently twisting them in opposite directions and easily remove the pit. If it is a clingstone, you will need to cut the flesh away from the pit.

Oranges. Sometimes things don't get much better in life than a glass of freshly squeezed orange juice. The big dose of immune-boosting vitamin C, sun-drenched flavor, and bright color should be everybody's everyday necessity. Oranges also contain pectin, which lowers cholesterol levels, and folic acid, important to pregnant women.

Selection: Look for oranges that are firm, but not hard, and have smooth skin. Those that feel heavy for their size will be the juiciest.

Preparation: For better taste and more nutrients, always use freshly squeezed, strained orange juice. Follow prep instructions for grapefruit.

Papayas. Sometimes called pawpaw, this beta carotene—rich fruit imparts a velvety texture to smoothies. Papayas contain papain, an enzyme that aids in digestion, making them a good remedy for an upset stomach. They are also a good source of vitamin C and potassium.

Selection: Look for papayas that are mostly yellow or orange and slightly soft to the touch. Pale green papayas are unripe and may not sweeten. Avoid papayas that are bruised, have soft spots, or show signs of mold.

Preparation: Refrigerate papayas only an hour or two before using. To prep for a smoothie, cut in half from stem to bottom. Scrape out the seeds, peel, and chop into half-inch pieces.

Peaches. A perfectly ripe, downy peach is one of the best and juiciest summertime experiences around. In the wintertime, frozen peaches will have to do to add a bright taste and thick texture to smoothies. Nutritionally, peaches are rich in beta carotene, vitamin C, and potassium.

Selection: One of the best indicators of ripeness is a rich peach aroma. Hard peaches should be avoided. A ripe peach will be firm yet give slightly to soft pressure, especially on its shoulder.

Preparation: Like nectarines, peaches fall into two categories—freestone or clingstone. To remove the stone, follow the prep instructions for nectarines. For smoothies, peaches should be peeled.

Pears. Pears fall into two categories: Asian pears are crunchy when ripe; European pears are soft, sweet, and juicy, making them perfect for smoothies. They're a good source of fiber, potassium, vitamins C and A, folic acid, and calcium.

Selection: A ripe pear will feel a little soft near the stem. Unlike most other fruits, they ripen best after they are harvested. Ripen at room temperature in a closed paper bag.

Preparation: Cut pear into quarters, remove the core and fibrous strings that run from the stem end to the core, and then peel with a paring knife.

Pineapple. In the days before air-shipping, only those living in tropical climates could enjoy the flavor of fresh, ripe pineapple. Now we're lucky in that ripe pineapples abound and at prices most of us can easily afford. Fresh pineapple provides loads of vitamin C and potassium. It is also an anti-inflammatory that can soothe a sore throat.

Selection: When a pineapple is fully ripe, a leaf can easily be pulled from its crown. The smell should be pleasantly fragrant; it should not smell of fermentation. Because pineapples do not continue to sweeten after they're picked, only air freight can deliver the sweetest specimens.

Preparation: With a sharp knife, cut off the crown of leaves, including a bit more of the top, then cut off the bottom.

Working all the way around the pineapple, make fairly thick cuts (about $1/8$ inch) from the top downward to remove the outer layer of skin in strips. Using the point of a vegetable peeler, dig out the eyes. Cut away the fibrous core; the remainder can then be cut into half-inch pieces.

Plums. The most diverse group of the stone fruits—ranging greatly in size, shape, color, and sweetness—plums are a good source of vitamins C and A, and potassium.

Selection: Look for plums that are plump and full-colored. Ripe plums will feel slightly soft to a light touch, and will be fragrant. Firm plums will soften, but not sweeten. Avoid very hard plums; they will never ripen.

Preparation: To remove the pit, cut around the plum, from stem to bottom on one side and then along the opposite side up to the top. If the plum is a freestone variety, the halves will separate easily. If it is a clingstone, you will need to cut the flesh away from the pit.

Prunes. The official name for prunes, since the new millennium, is dried plums, though in this book I still refer to them as prunes. What hasn't changed is the fact that tasty prunes are really good for you. Famous as a laxative owing to their high fiber content, they're also rich in iron, potassium, calcium, beta carotene, and vitamin C.

Preparation: Soak chopped prunes in hot water for 15 minutes to soften.

Raisins. About one-half of the world's supply of raisins comes from the San Joaquin Valley of California, where the raisin production took off in the 1870s after a heat wave dried the grape crop on the vine—proof of the power of American ingenuity. Raisins add flavor, fiber, and sweetness to smoothies. They are a good source of iron, potassium, and some vitamin B and A.

Preparation: Raisins are small enough to add to smoothies without softening in water. However, if you want the flavor of raisins but with less sugar, soak them for a bit.

Raspberries. The key to truly enjoying the ruby-red gems of the berry world is to buy only raspberries that are grown close to home and in season. Raspberries are a source of magnesium, vitamins C and B_6, potassium, folic acid, and calcium.

Selection: Raspberries should be plump and free of mold, which usually begins in the stem.

Preparation: Raspberries are often too delicate to be washed—which is a good reason to buy berries from an organic farmer who does not use pesticides. As quickly as possible, berries should be removed from their container and placed in a single layer on a paper towel-lined tray.

Strawberries. Strawberries are a classic smoothie ingredient, adding delicious flavor and a pretty pink color. They are higher in vitamin C than any other berry, and are also rich in potassium, calcium, manganese, and antioxidants. Highly perishable when ripe, strawberries should be bought locally whenever possible. Cultivated strawberries fall into two categories: June-bearing and ever-bearing types. The first has one bumper crop in late spring or early summer. The second produces several smaller crops throughout the summer and into autumn.

Selection: Look for plump, richly colored berries with shiny skins.

Preparation: If you've bought organic strawberries, there is no need to wash them, unless they are sandy or have soil attached to them. Once home, lay berries in a single layer on a shallow, paper towel-lined tray.

Watermelon. This sweet, juicy, and refreshing melon has a longer history of cultivation than any other melon, being enjoyed in Egypt since before 2000 B.C. A good source of potassium and vitamin C, watermelon is also rich in electrolytes, which are lost when you sweat, making it a perfect fruit to enjoy after exercise.

Selection: Though watermelon seeds are edible, most of us won't want them in a smoothie, so look for a seedless watermelon. When judging if a watermelon is ripe, look at the bottom end where it rested on the ground. It should be yellow, not pale green or white. Also, watermelon skin should appear dull rather than glossy, and be without bruises.

Preparation: If you do need to seed a watermelon, first cut it in half, then in quarters. Cut a diagonal slice just above the seed line on both sides of the wedge. Remove the seedless wedge and set aside. Next, cut along the bottom of the seed line on both sides of the wedge. Remove the strip of flesh that is full of seeds and discard. The remaining seeds can be removed with the tip of a knife or a spoon. To remove the remaining melon from rind, cut the quartered wedges into smaller, more manageable pieces, about 1 1/2 to 2 inches in width. Run a knife along the rind to separate the flesh. The seedless flesh of the watermelon can now be cut into cubes.

Vegetables

Avocados. Though botanically a fruit, the rich, buttery, nutty-flavored avocado is usually put to savory uses, and so we think of it as a vegetable. Avocados develop a very high fat content and ripen only after they've been picked. The two most common avocados are the Hass (dark-green, nearly black, pebbly-skinned) and the Fuerte (more pear-shaped with medium-green and smoother, thinner skin). Hass avocados have the richer taste and creamier texture. All avocados are abundant sources of potassium, folic acid, vitamin E, and a very healthy fat called oleic acid, making them a good choice for people who need to put on weight without adding saturated fats.

Selection: Avocados are ripe when they give slightly to the touch, especially at the stem end. To ripen avocados at home, buy them when they're still quite firm to lessen the chance of purchasing bruised merchandise, and place in a paper bag.

Preparation: Cut the avocado in half lengthwise. Remove the pit, and scoop out the flesh. Since avocado flesh quickly turns brown once it is exposed to air, it's best to use an avocado soon after you've cut into it. Vinegar or citrus juice will help slow the browning process.

Beets. Beets have a bold and breathtakingly beautiful color, the highest sugar content of any vegetable, and powerful blood-cleansing properties. If drunk too often, beet juice can upset a stomach, so it's best not to drink a beet-inspired smoothie every day. Beets contain calcium, sulfur, iron, potassium, choline, beta carotene, and vitamin C. They're also high in folic acid, which helps prevent birth defects.

Selection: Look for beets that have firm, finely textured skin. Avoid beets that are soft or shriveled. Tops should be a vibrant green, showing no signs of wilting or yellowing.

Preparation: Unpeeled beets—and their greens—can be juiced. Scrub well, cut off both ends of the beet, and discard greens that look wilted or have a yellowish tinge. Cut beets into manageable pieces for your juicer.

Carrots. Of all the orange-colored fruits and vegetables, carrots are the highest in beta carotene, which helps our bodies fight disease. Carrot juice is also an excellent source of vitamins C and B_6, folic acid, magnesium, and potassium. Carrot juice has a sweet, mild flavor that is enjoyable on its own—unlike other vegetable juices that are better mixed with fruit juices. Carrot juice is usually available at natural food stores, though juicing your own will be tastier and provide more nutrients.

Selection: Look for firm carrots; they should be crisp and difficult to bend. Their skin should be smooth and without blemishes, and the tops should be green, not wilted or blackened.

Preparation: Scrub well, cut off both ends of the carrot, and cut into manageable pieces.

Celery. Celery's clean, bright, and naturally salty taste complements other vegetable juices with heavier components. Celery juice is cleansing and has diuretic properties, and is a good source of potassium, folic acid, manganese, vitamin B_6, calcium, sodium, and especially vitamin C.

Selection: Look for firm, closely formed bunches with crisp, green leaves.

Preparation: Both the stalk and leaves can be juiced. Scrub well and remove wilted leaves.

Cucumbers. Tasty and refreshing, a frosty cucumber-based smoothie will revive you on a hot summer day. Seedless cucumbers are a good choice for smoothies, as it can be a hassle to remove the seeds.

Selection: Look for firm cucumbers with bright color. The smaller cucumber of each type will generally have the smallest seeds.

Preparation: To prepare for use in smoothies, peel and cut in half lengthwise. Using a paring knife, make two diagonal cuts just below and on either side of the seed line and discard the seed-filled wedge. Chop the remaining flesh.

Red Bell Peppers. Red bell peppers are a good source of vitamins C and B_6, and, like other orange- or red-colored fruits and vegetables, rich in beta carotene.

Selection: Look for peppers that have shiny skin that is smooth and unwrinkled. Peppers should be heavy for their size, and their stems should be fresh and green.

Preparation: Scrub the pepper, then cut lengthwise into flat panels, discarding the stem, core, and seeds. It can then be chopped into smaller pieces for smoothies.

Scallions. A mild member of the pungent allium family, scallions (also called green onions or spring onions) provide a hint of zesty onion flavor to savory smoothies. Scallions' green tops provide vitamin C, folic acid, calcium, and beta carotene. They are also a very good source of vitamins A and K, iron, potassium, and manganese.

Selection: Look for crisp-looking tops with rich green color and unmarred, white bottoms.

Preparation: Trim wilted parts from the green ends and the rootlets from the bulb end.

Tomatoes. The tomato is actually a fruit, though we use it like a vegetable. Tomatoes are an excellent source of vitamin C and potassium, and they are one of the best sources of lycopene, a carotenoid that is helpful in the prevention of prostate cancer and heart disease.

Selection: Tomatoes should be plump and heavy for their size, with smooth skins. Avoid tomatoes with blemishes, bruises, or deep cracks.

Preparation: To prepare for smoothies, place in boiling water for 15 seconds, then transfer to ice water. Cut out the stem ends; their skins should slide off easily. Cut in half crosswise, squeeze out their seeds, and chop.

Nuts and Seeds

Along with contributing healthy protein and fat to smoothies, nuts and seeds contain iron, zinc, calcium, potassium, and a number of trace elements. Some nuts and seeds have additional and unique health benefits, and each has a distinct flavor. For use in smoothies, all nuts and seeds, including peanut butter, should be unsalted and unsweetened.

Almonds. Along with being one of the richest sources of calcium in the vegetable kingdom, almonds are rich in potassium, phosphorus, magnesium, iron, zinc, folic acid, niacin, and vitamins E and A.

Flax Seed. This small, glossy seed is rich in essential fatty acids (both omega-3 and omega-6), and is one of the richest sources of lignans, a plant estrogen that has antiviral, antibacteria, antifungal, antioxidant, and immune-enhancing properties. Flax seed should be ground to release its essential oils; do this in a coffee grinder, then refrigerate or freeze to prevent rancidity.

Hazelnuts. These delicious nuts have been eaten by humans since earliest times. Though not nutritional powerhouses relative to some other nuts, hazelnuts are a good source of calcium, iron, and zinc, and they are lower in fat than most nuts.

Macadamia Nuts. Notoriously difficult to extract from their shells, shelled macadamia nuts fetch a high price. But their delicate, creamy flavor and crisp texture make them worth every penny. Though higher in fat than most nuts, rich-tasting macadamias are a good source of potassium, phosphorus, magnesium, calcium, and folic acid.

Peanut Butter. Found in 75 percent of American homes, many consider peanut butter to be the perfect food. Peanuts have more protein than any other nut, and are rich in iron. They are high in heart-healthy fats, and a good source of potassium, phosphorus, magnesium, calcium, selenium, niacin, vitamin E, and especially folic acid.

Pecans. A favorite native nut in the United States, especially in the South, mild, slightly sweet pecans are a source of potassium, phosphorus, magnesium, calcium, zinc, iron, folic acid, and vitamin A.

Pistachios. Compared with other nuts, pistachios are low in fat and contain a high level of potassium. They are also a good source of vitamin B_6, thiamine, phosphorus, magnesium, copper, and especially vitamin A, iron, and calcium.

Pumpkin Seeds. These delicious little morsels with a rich, somewhat peanuty flavor are abundant in protein and iron, and are also a good source of potassium, magnesium, phosphorus, calcium, zinc, and heart-healthy fats.

Tahini. This creamy, rich-tasting sesame-seed paste is a good source of essential fatty acids, iron, calcium, potassium, thiamine, magnesium, phosphorus, zinc, iron, copper, manganese, and some protein. The hulled type (light ivory colored) is usually superior in taste to the unhulled type (darker in color). However, unhulled tahini has more vitamins and protein.

Walnuts. These tasty nuts rise above the nut crowd with their very high levels of alpha linolenic acid, an omega-3. Walnuts are also a good source of potassium, phosphorus, magnesium, folic acid, calcium, iron, copper, and especially manganese.

Other Nutritional Supplements & Secret Ingredients

Bran. This traditional breakfast ingredient is the outer layer of a wheat, oat, or rice grain. Like prunes, bran has a less than glamorous reputation—often thought of as being "good for you." Yet bran has a sweet, nutty flavor that is welcome in most smoothies. Along with being a great source of fiber, bran is rich in iron, magnesium, phosphorus, potassium, zinc, copper, thiamine, riboflavin, niacin, and vitamin B_6. Bran will change the texture of a smoothie, so start with 1 tablespoon or less.

Brewer's Yeast. This supplement is a great source of the B vitamins and chromium, which are necessary for energy production. It is also a good source of copper, selenium, and magnesium. Another option for boosting vitamin B levels is to use liquid vitamin B complex; however, lacking folic acid and minerals, it is not as nutritional as brewer's yeast. Brewer's yeast has a distinct flavor that can overpower other ingredients, so start by adding a small amount.

Cocoa Power and Chocolate Syrup. Sometimes nothing else will do except a thick chocolate-flavored smoothie. That's where cocoa powder and chocolate syrup come in. Cocoa powder has less than half the calories of chocolate syrup; the downside is that it can impart a bitter taste if you use more than 1 tablespoon. One solution is to use 1 part cocoa powder and 1 part chocolate syrup.

Coconut Milk. This naturally sweet milk adds a delicious tropical flavor to smoothies. Look for light, unsweetened coconut milk. Do not confuse coconut milk with the high-calorie sweetened cream of coconut, typically used in rich desserts and piña coladas.

Extracts, Natural. Herbal or plant extracts, in powder or liquid form, are reputed to possess distinct medicinal benefits. Though not approved by the FDA, they should be treated with respect as powerful medicines. Children, pregnant women, or anyone taking prescription drugs shouldn't take them without consulting a physician. Also, never use more than the dosage recommended. None of these supplements should be taken in high doses over a long period of time.

Ginkgo Biloba. Made from the leaves of the ginkgo biloba tree, it is used to increase blood flow to the brain, improving alertness, memory, and concentration.

Ginseng. This large taproot has been used for centuries in Asia as a tonic, stimulator, and rejuvenator. It is reputed to boost the immune system, help relieve stress and lethargy, treat impotence and infertility, and counter PMS and menopause symptoms. Hypoglycemia patients should avoid high amounts of ginseng.

Seasonal Chart

Spring

(mid-March to mid-June)

Avocados	Limes
Apricots	Mangoes
Bananas	Oranges
Blueberries	Papayas
Carrots	Pineapple
Celery	Plums
Cherries	Raspberries
Grapefruit	Scallions
Kiwifruit	Strawberries
Lemons	

Summer

(mid-June to mid-September)

Apples	Limes
Apricots	Mangoes
Avocados	Melons
Bananas	Nectarines
Beets	Oranges
Blackberries	Papayas
Blueberries	Peaches
Carrots	Pears
Celery	Pineapple
Cherries	Plums
Cucumbers	Raspberries
Figs	Scallions
Grapefruit	Strawberries
Grapes	Sweet Peppers
Lemons	Tomatoes

Autumn

(mid-September to mid-December)

Apples	Lemons
Avocados	Limes
Bananas	Oranges
Beets	Papayas
Carrots	Pears
Celery	Pineapple
Cranberries	Plums
Figs	Pomegranates
Grapefruit	Raspberries
Grapes	Sweet Peppers
Kiwifruit	

Winter

(mid-December to mid-March)

Apples	Kiwifruit
Avocados	Lemons
Bananas	Limes
Beets	Oranges
Carrots	Papayas
Celery	Pears
Cranberries	Pineapple
Grapefruit	

Licorice Root. This herb has been used for thousands of years in Asia for a variety of ailments and discomforts, including treating stomach ulcers and arthritis pain, reducing liver damage, and alleviating PMS symptoms.

Milk Thistle. Milk thistle has been used since Roman times to treat liver problems. It helps to protect the liver by preventing damage from a variety of poisons. Milk thistle is also a powerful antioxidant.

Ginger, Fresh. The spicy flavor of grated gingerroot accents all sorts of sweet and savory smoothies. In addition to its great taste, ginger is renowned for its curative powers of treating motion sickness, nausea, and pregnancy's morning sickness.

Mint, Fresh. Along with adding a lovely "minty-fresh" flavor to smoothies, mint aids digestion and is helpful in preventing nausea and morning sickness.

Protein Powder. Protein powder provides your body with this essential nutrient—without the saturated fat that comes with animal products—and helps to nutritionally balance carbohydrates. The many varieties of protein powder are made from cow's milk, goat's milk, eggs, or soy beans. I recommend plain soy protein powder: plain, because it's more versatile; soy, because you'll get all the added benefits of soy (their isoflavones, for example).

Spirulina. The most popular of several algae that are grown for use as supplements, spirulina is an excellent source of chlorophyll. It is also said to contain high amounts of protein, vitamins, minerals, and beta carotene. Algae has a distinct seaweed and saltwater flavor, so add spirulina in small increments.

Vanilla Extract. It's hard to go wrong by adding a few drops of this most complementary of flavors to a fruit smoothie. Besides adding a delicious accent to most fruits, vanilla may be good for your love life: There is some evidence that it may stimulate the motor nerves used in sexual response.

Wheat Germ. Slightly nutty and sweet, the delicious flavor of fiber-rich wheat germ is a great addition to any smoothie. Wheat germ is one of the best natural sources of vitamin E, and it's chock-full of thiamine, riboflavin, vitamin B_6, folic acid, iron, magnesium, selenium, and zinc.

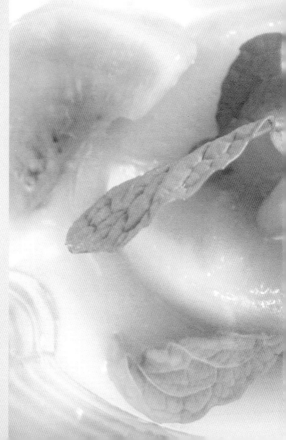

Body Beautiful

chapter

1

Cherries Jubilee

Makes 16 ounces.
Per 8-ounce serving:
About 185 calories,
4g protein, 20g carbo-
hydrates, 11g total fat
(7g saturated),
4g fiber, 0mg choles-
terol, 17mg sodium

*Once in a while, even smoothie drinkers
concerned with slimming down should
treat themselves to flavor-packed cherries.
Though higher in carbohydrates than
some fruit, cherries are a great source of
vitamins A and C, and magnesium.*

3/4 cup sliced mango

3/4 cup soy milk

1/4 cup frozen cherries

1/4 cup unsweetened coconut milk

1 tablespoon almond paste

Green Tea Slimmer

Makes 16 ounces.
Per 8-ounce serving:
About 46 calories,
1g protein, 12g carbo-
hydrates, trace fat
(trace saturated),
2g fiber, 0mg choles-
terol, 11mg sodium

*Along with providing antioxidants,
green tea stimulates metabolism, helping
to burn fat.*

4 frozen cubes strongly brewed green tea

1/2 cup chilled strongly brewed green tea

3/4 cup chopped honeydew melon

1 kiwifruit, peeled and chopped

2 to 3 drops stevia, or to taste

Mexican Chocolate Crush

Makes 16 ounces
Per 8-ounce serving:
About 115 calories,
7g protein, 16g carbo-
hydrates, 3g total fat
(2g saturated),
2g fiber, 10mg choles-
terol, 88mg sodium

When you can't hold back your chocolate cravings any longer, whip up a low-fat smoothie with South-of-the-border flair. Cayenne and chocolate stimulate metabolism.

4 frozen cubes low-fat milk

1/2 cup low-fat milk

1/2 cup frozen low-fat vanilla yogurt

2 tablespoons unsweetened cocoa powder

1/2 teaspoon vanilla extract

1/4 teaspoon ground cinnamon

Generous pinch cayenne pepper

Pinch black pepper

2 to 3 drops stevia, or to taste

Blushing

Peach tinted with a blush of pink strawberry makes this smoothie as pretty as it is slimming. Peaches and strawberries are especially low in carbohydrates, and the dairy gives your body much-needed fat and protein, holding hunger at bay and providing energy.

Peach

Makes 16 ounces.
Per 8-ounce serving:
About 103 calories,
6g protein, 16g carbo-
hydrates, 2g total fat
(1g saturated), 2g fiber,
9mg cholesterol,
74mg sodium

3/4 cup frozen sliced peaches

1/2 cup low-fat yogurt

1/2 low-fat milk

1/4 cup frozen strawberries

Pinch ground cinnamon

2 to 3 drops stevia, or to taste

Passion-
Pineapple
Crush

Makes 16 ounces.
Per 8-ounce serving:
About 78 calories,
1g protein, 20g carbo-
hydrates, trace fat
(trace saturated),
4g fiber, 0mg choles-
terol, 4mg sodium

This tropical-inspired smoothie tastes great and is good for you, too. Passion fruit is rich in potassium, calcium, folic acid, vitamin A, and niacin (also known as vitamin B$_3$). Among a host of other good deeds, niacin helps maintain healthy skin and helps in the metabolism of carbs, fats, and proteins.

$1/2$ banana

$1/2$ cup diced pineapple

$1/4$ cup passion fruit juice

6 ice cubes

Pink Melon Crush

This fat-free, low-calorie smoothie is a refreshing, naturally sweet treat—perfect to satisfy a sweet tooth.

Makes 16 ounces.
Per 8-ounce serving:
About 63 calories, 1g protein, 15g carbohydrates, trace total fat (trace saturated), 2g fiber, 0mg cholesterol, 7mg sodium

1/2 cup freshly squeezed orange juice

1/2 cup strawberries

1/4 cantaloupe, chopped

6 ice cubes

Ginger Tea Slimmer

Both ginger and green tea increase metabolism, helping your body burn fat.

Makes 16 ounces.
Per 8-ounce serving:
About 56 calories, 1g protein, 15g carbohydrates, trace total fat (trace saturated), 2g fiber, 0mg cholesterol, 4mg sodium

3/4 cup chilled strongly brewed green tea

3/4 cup frozen sliced peaches

1/2 cup sliced mango

Generous pinch freshly grated gingerroot

5 to 6 drops stevia, or to taste

Grapefruit Crush

Makes 16 ounces.
Per 8-ounce serving:
About 80 calories,
1g protein, 20g carbo-
hydrates, trace fat
(trace saturated),
1g fiber, 0mg choles-
terol, 2mg sodium

Grapefruit has long been thought to kick-start metabolism and help the body burn fat. There was even a popular grapefruit diet in the 1980s—at the time considered a passing fad. Recent studies have shown that adding grapefruit to your diet (with each meal) can aid weight loss.

3/4 cup freshly squeezed grapefruit juice

1/2 cup frozen sliced nectarine

1/2 cup sliced mango

4 ice cubes

Lean Machine

Makes 16 ounces.
Per 8-ounce serving:
About 93 calories,
7g protein, 11g carbo-
hydrates, 3g fat (trace
saturated), 4g fiber,
0mg cholesterol,
26mg sodium

Protein is needed to burn fat, and dieters—not only muscle builders—need protein too!

1 cup soy milk or low-fat dairy milk

1/2 cup frozen strawberries

1/2 cup diced papaya

2 tablespoons protein powder

2 to 3 drops stevia, or to taste

Bran Fat Buster

Makes 16 ounces.
Per 8-ounce serving:
About 105 calories,
5g protein, 17g carbo-
hydrates, 3g total fat
(2g saturated fat),
3g fiber, 10mg choles-
terol, 62mg sodium

Wheat bran is a good source of chromium, an essential mineral that is thought to reduce body fat. Dairy products also have trace amounts of this fat-busting mineral. And the fiber in bran will help keep you satiated longer since it increases the time the smoothie spends in your stomach.

1 cup low-fat milk

1/2 cup frozen strawberries

1/2 cup frozen sliced nectarines

1/4 cup frozen blueberries

1 tablespoon wheat bran

Pinch ground cinnamon

2 to 3 drops stevia, or to taste

Orange

Zero-calorie orange blossom water adds an exotic and delicate touch to smoothies. The scent of orange and fresh mint will transport you to a flowering courtyard in Marrakech.

Blossom Smoothie

Makes 16 ounces.
Per 8-ounce serving:
About 113 calories,
4g protein, 24g carbo-
hydrates, 1g total fat
(1g saturated), 2g fiber,
4mg cholesterol,
44mg sodium

3/4 cup sliced mango

3/4 cup frozen sliced peaches

1/2 cup plain low-fat yogurt

2 tablespoons freshly squeezed
    orange juice

1/2 teaspoon orange blossom water

2 to 3 fresh mint leaves

2 to 3 drops stevia, or to taste

Nuts for Pistachios

Makes 16 ounces.

Per 8-ounce serving:
About 170 calories,
5g protein, 15g carbo-
hydrates, 11g total fat
(8g saturated), 2g fiber,
7mg cholesterol,
52mg sodium

Nuts and dairy prroducts are sources of chromium, a mineral that may help burn body fat. Pistachios are unique among nuts in their high level of carotenoids, which help the body fight cancer-causing substances. Another bonus—in the world of nuts, pistachios are low in calories.

3/4 cup low-fat milk

1/2 cup frozen diced pineapple

1/2 cup diced papaya

1/4 cup low-fat unsweetened
    coconut milk

1 to 2 tablespoons pistachios

Blast–Off Smoothies

chapter

2

Almond

Rice milk (higher in carbs than dairy or soy milk) and almonds add a twist to the classic banana-strawberry combination. This terrific source of carbohydrates, fat, and protein will give you extra energy and staying power to meet your goals for the day.

Crunch

Makes 16 ounces.
Per 8-ounce serving:
About 178 calories,
3g protein, 31g carbo-
hydrates, 6g total fat
(trace saturated),
3g fiber, 0mg choles-
terol, 48mg sodium

1 frozen banana

1 cup rice milk

1/2 cup frozen strawberries

2 tablespoons almonds

Iron Strength

Makes 16 ounces.
Per 8-ounce serving:
About 208 calories,
6g protein, 43g car-
bohydrates, 3g total
fat (1g saturated),
6g fiber, 2mg choles-
terol, 38mg sodium

*Iron plays a vital role in transplanting
oxygen, via red blood cells, to where
it's most needed in the body. If you're
lacking energy, you may need more iron
in your diet, as iron deficiency is one of
the most common causes of fatigue.*

1 frozen banana

6 pitted dates, soaked in warm water
    for 15 minutes to soften, chopped

1 1/4 cups soy milk

1/4 cup plain yogurt

Pinch nutmeg

Variation: For richness and additional
protein, add 1 teaspoon almond paste.

Vitamin B Replenisher

Makes 16 ounces.
Per 8-ounce serving:
About 119 calories,
6g protein, 18g carbo-
hydrates, 3g total fat
(1g saturated),
2g fiber, 7mg choles-
terol, 49mg sodium

The B vitamins, and especially B_1 and B_3, provide energy. Many athletes have low B_6 levels. This vitamin B–rich refresher will give you an energy lift and, if you work out regularly, replenish B_6.

3/4 cup milk

1/2 cup frozen strawberries

1/2 cup sliced mango

1/4 cup silken tofu

2 tablespoons apple juice

1 tablespoon wheat germ

1 drop liquid vitamin B complex

Blueberry

Oat milk is especially high in carbohydrates, which are the body's number one source of energy. Oats also help to maintain blood sugar levels, which helps alleviate mood swings and sudden slumps in energy.

Boost

Makes 16 ounces.
Per 8-ounce serving:
About 158 calories,
3g protein, 34g carbo-
hydrates, 2g total fat
(trace saturated),
4g fiber, 0mg choles-
terol, 55mg sodium

1 frozen banana

3/4 cup oat milk

1/2 cup frozen blueberries

1/4 cup rice milk

2 tablespoons concentrated apple juice

1 tablespoon wheat germ

The Chocolate

Here's a delicious way to satisfy your sweet tooth while replenishing spent nutrients after a workout

Reward

Makes 16 ounces.
Per 8-ounce serving:
About 272 calories,
14g protein, 26g carbo-
hydrates, 13g total fat
(5g saturated), 2g fiber,
18mg cholesterol,
116mg sodium

1 frozen banana

1 cup milk

$1/2$ cup plain yogurt

2 tablespoons unsweetened unsalted
    peanut butter

2 tablespoons protein powder

1 tablespoon unsweetened cocoa powder

2 teaspoons chocolate syrup

For the Long Haul

Makes 16 ounces.
Per 8-ounce serving:
170 calories, 6g protein, 26g carbohydrates, 6g total fat (1g saturated), 4g fiber, 0mg cholesterol, 28mg sodium

The glucose in this smoothie will release slowly, giving you sustained energy.

3/4 cup frozen cherries

1/2 cup soy milk

1/4 cup apple juice

1/4 cup pear juice

1/4 cup silken tofu

1 tablespoon almond paste

Mineral Boost

Makes 16 ounces.
Per 8-ounce serving:
About 177 calories, 6g protein, 29g carbohydrates, 6g total fat (2g saturated), 3g fiber, 10mg cholesterol, 61mg sodium

A lack of magnesium can cause fatigue and weak muscles, and exercise can deplete potassium levels. This smoothie is rich in both minerals.

1 frozen banana

3/4 cup milk or enriched soy milk

3/4 cup frozen cherries

1 to 2 tablespoons pecans or nut
   of choice

Quick Boost

Makes 16 ounces.
Per 8-ounce serving:
About 163 calories,
7g protein, 31g carbo-
hydrates, 2g total fat
(1g saturated), 1g fiber,
7mg cholesterol,
93mg sodium

Glucose—derived from carbohydrates and stored as glycogen in the liver and muscles—is the only form of carbohydrate used directly by muscles for energy. During most exercise, our store of glycogen isn't used up, but some athletes eat or drink carbohydrates during exercise to help maintain their glucose and energy levels.

For a speedy burst of energy before working out, drink this smoothie, which is filled with quick-burning glucose.

1 frozen banana

1/2 to 3/4 cup frozen vanilla yogurt

1/4 cup carrot-orange juice

1 teaspoon honey

2 to 3 tablespoons milk, to thin

Pinch nutmeg

Peanut
Butter
Lover

Carbohydrates and fat are the main sources of energy for our body, and fiber helps our body metabolize carbohydrates over a longer period of time. Naturally filled with all three of these nutrients, a glass of PB Lover will sustain your body for hours.

Makes 16 ounces.
Per 8-ounce serving:
About 217 calories, 9g protein, 24g carbohydrates, 11g total fat (3g saturated), 3g fiber, 4mg cholesterol, 27mg sodium

1 frozen banana

1/2 cup soy milk

1/4 cup plain yogurt

1/4 cup silken tofu

2 tablespoons peanut butter

1 tablespoon raisins

Best Results

Makes 16 ounces.
Per 8-ounce serving:
About 117 calories,
7g protein, 16g carbo-
hydrates, 4g total fat
(trace saturated),
4g fiber, 0mg choles-
terol, 25mg sodium

If you're serious about building muscle, this protein and flaxseed–paired smoothie is for you. Protein builds muscle, and the omega-3 fatty acids in flaxseed lock protein into muscle fibers.

1 cup soy or dairy milk

1/2 frozen banana

1/4 cup frozen blueberries

1/4 cup frozen sliced peaches

2 tablespoons protein powder

1 tablespoon apple juice

1 teaspoon ground flaxseed

Smoothies for Women

Celery Cure

Makes 16 ounces.
Per 8-ounce serving:
About 57 calories,
2g protein, 13g carbo-
hydrates, trace total
fat (trace saturated),
4g fiber, 0mg choles-
terol, 216mg sodium

*Water retention is often a symptom of
PMS or menopause. Celery, a mild
diuretic, will help.*

1 cup carrot juice

1/2 cup apple juice

1/4 cup celery juice

1/8 teaspoon freshly grated gingerroot

With Child

Makes 16 ounces.
Per 8-ounce serving:
About 173 calories,
6g protein, 28g carbo-
hydrates, 5g total
fat (3g saturated),
2g fiber, 16mg choles-
terol, 62mg sodium

*Rich in folic acid, a B vitamin proven
to reduce the chance of birth defects, this
smoothie is a good addition to a pregnant
woman's diet.*

3/4 cup soy milk

1/2 cup frozen strawberries

1/2 cup diced papaya

1/4 cup plain yogurt

2 tablespoons orange juice

Beets for Baby

Makes 16 ounces.
Per 8-ounce serving:
About 82 calories,
1g protein, 22g carbo-
hydrates, trace total
fat (trace saturated),
1g fiber, 0mg choles-
terol, 31mg sodium

Beets are plentiful in folic acid, which prevents birth defects of the brain and spinal cord when taken very early in pregnancy. To experience its full effects, women should take folic acid daily the month prior to becoming pregnant and during the first month of pregnancy. Another bonus for women: Folic acid may help protect against cervical cancer.

1 cup carrot juice

$1/4$ cup beet juice

$1/4$ cup apple juice

$1/4$ cup pear juice

1 teaspoon freshly squeezed lemon juice

Pinch freshly grated gingerroot

Vitamin

If you take an oral contraceptive, you may be deficient in vitamin B. This vitamin B– rich smoothie will help replenish your body's stores.

B Helper

Makes 16 ounces.
Per 8-ounce serving:
About 187 calories,
5g protein, 34g carbo-
hydrates, 5g total fat
(2g saturated),
4g fiber, 8mg choles-
terol, 104mg sodium

3/4 cup frozen pitted cherries

1/2 frozen banana

1/2 cup plain yogurt

1/2 cup almond milk

1 tablespoon wheat germ

1 drop liquid vitamin B complex

The PMS Solution

Help is on the way! Mint is said to relieve cramps, and chocolate releases pleasurable endorphins that help to counteract the general unpleasantness of PMS.

Makes 16 ounces.
Per 8-ounce serving:
About 203 calories,
7g protein, 33g carbo-
hydrates, 6g total fat
(3g saturated), 2g fiber,
16mg cholesterol,
95mg sodium

1 cup chocolate soy milk

3/4 cup frozen pitted cherries

1/2 cup plain yogurt

1 tablespoon chocolate syrup

1/4 teaspoon vanilla extract

2 or 3 fresh mint leaves

Mint leaf, to garnish

Strawdairy

Makes 16 ounces.
Per 8-ounce serving:
About 181 calories,
6g protein, 30g carbo-
hydrates, 5g total fat
(3g saturated),
4g fiber, 18mg choles-
terol, 73mg sodium

This dairy-based smoothie is perfect for pregnant and lactating women, who need extra vitamin B_{12}.

3/4 cup milk

3/4 cup frozen strawberries

1/2 frozen banana

1/4 cup plain yogurt

1/4 cup frozen raspberries

2 tablespoons apple juice

1 drop liquid B complex

Green Tea Girl

Makes 16 ounces.
Per 8-ounce serving:
About 98 calories,
4g protein, 17g carbo-
hydrates, 3g total fat
(trace saturated),
4g fiber, 0mg choles-
terol, 19mg sodium

Green tea and soy milk have phytoestro-gens (an estrogenlike plant compound), which may help relieve women of menopausal symptoms, such as hot flashes, anxiety, and mood swings.

6 frozen cubes strongly brewed green
tea, or 3/4 cup chilled green tea

1 ripe pear, peeled, cored, and chopped

3/4 cup soy milk

2 tablespoons pear juice

Pinch freshly grated gingerroot

Honeymooner's Elixir

Makes 16 ounces.
Per 8-ounce serving:
About 154 calories,
3g protein, 33g carbo-
hydrates, 2g total fat
(trace saturated),
3g fiber, 0mg choles-
terol, 16mg sodium

*Fifty percent of women will have a
urinary tract infection at least once in
their lifetime. Cranberries offer protection
against this painful infection, sometimes
known as "honeymooner's disease."*

1 frozen banana

3/4 cup soy milk

1/4 cup cranberry juice

1/4 cup frozen red raspberries

2 tablespoons apple juice

2 tablespoons pear juice

2 tablespoons dried cranberries, soaked
in warm water for 15 minutes
to soften

Peachy

Rich in calcium, dairy-based smoothies help build bone mass and may help prevent osteoporosis.

Keen

Makes 16 ounces.
Per 8-ounce serving:
About 216 calories,
6g protein, 41g carbo-
hydrates, 4g total
fat (2g saturated),
3g fiber, 13mg choles-
terol, 77mg sodium

$3/4$ cup plain yogurt

$3/4$ cup frozen sliced peaches

$1/4$ cup frozen blueberries

$1/4$ cup milk

2 tablespoons honey

$1/4$ teaspoon vanilla extract

Woman's All-Purpose Helpmate

Makes 16 ounces.
Per 8-ounce serving:
About 143 calories,
6g protein, 20g carbo-
hydrates, 5g total fat
(1g saturated), 4g fiber,
0mg cholesterol,
66mg sodium

*Don't be afraid to pull out all the stops.
Chocolate releases endorphins, helping to
counter menstrual discomfort. Flaxseed
is a wonderful source of fiber and
isoflavones, both of which are beneficial
to women's health (isoflavones appear to
have estrogenlike effects in the body). In
addition, the soy in tofu may help with
the symptoms of menopause.*

1 1/4 cups chocolate soy milk

1/2 cup frozen strawberries

1/4 cup silken tofu

1 tablespoon ground flaxseed

Note: For a more chocolaty smoothie,
add a tablespoon of chocolate syrup.

Smoothies for Men

Mango Man

Pumpkin seeds are good for every-one, but especially men. Not only do they help reduce cholesterol and prevent coronary and other heart diseases, but they're also used to treat prostate enlargement.

Makes 16 ounces.
Per 8-ounce serving:
About 176 calories, 3g protein, 33g carbohydrates, 4g total fat (1g saturated), 2g fiber, 0mg cholesterol, 11mg sodium

3/4 cup rice milk

1/2 cup sliced mango

1/2 cup frozen blueberries

2 tablespoons guava juice

2 tablespoons pumpkin seeds

Saucy Mary

Makes 16 ounces.
Per 8-ounce serving:
About 116 calories,
3g protein, 29g carbo-
hydrates, 1g total fat
(trace saturated),
8g fiber, 0mg choles-
terol, 780mg sodium

*Lycopene, one of the multitude of disease-
fighting carotenoids, may prevent prostate
cancer. Tomatoes and processed tomato
products are especially rich in lycopene.*

1 1/2 cups chilled tomato juice,
   or 1/2 pound ripe tomatoes, peeled
   and seeded

1/2 cup ice

2 tablespoons celery juice (or 1 celery
   stalk, trimmed and chopped)

1 tablespoon freshly squeezed lemon juice

1/4 teaspoon grated fresh horseradish

2 to 3 dashes Worcestershire sauce

2 to 3 dashes hot pepper sauce

Pinch salt

Pinch pepper

Libido Enhancer

Makes 16 ounces.
Per 8-ounce serving:
About 88 calories,
1g protein, 22g carbo-
hydrates, trace total
fat (trace saturated),
trace fiber, 0mg cho-
lesterol, 3mg sodium

Ginseng has long been thought to increase sex drive and energy in general. Its slightly bitter flavor is masked by honey and spices here. If you still find the ginseng flavor too strong, add another tablespoon of honey.

6 frozen cubes black tea

1/4 cup chilled black tea

1/2 cup freshly squeezed orange juice

1 tablespoon honey

Pinch ground cloves

Pinch ground cinnamon

Pinch orange rind zest

Ginseng extract, use amount as
     package directs

Prowess

Licorice root is said to be a libido enhancer.

Plus

Makes 16 ounces.
Per 8-ounce serving:
About 234 calories,
6g protein, 44g carbo-
hydrates, 6g total fat
(3g saturated), 3g fiber,
16mg cholesterol,
133mg sodium

$1/2$ frozen banana

4 dates, soaked in water for 20 minutes
    to soften

1 cup almond milk

1 cup plain yogurt

2 teaspoons honey

Pinch ground cinnamon

Pinch ground cardamom

Licorice root extract, use amount as
    package directs

Baby-Making Formula

Makes 16 ounces.
Per 8-ounce serving:
About 216 calories,
8g protein, 25g carbo-
hydrates, 11g total fat
(3g saturated), 3g fiber,
8mg cholesterol,
35mg sodium

Vitamin E and zinc are said to help with men's fertility.

1 cup soy milk

$1/2$ cup plain yogurt

1 frozen banana

1 tablespoon peanut butter

1 tablespoon wheat germ

1 tablespoon concentrated apple juice

Aphrodisiac

Makes 16 ounces.
Per 8-ounce serving:
About 96 calories,
5g protein, 11g carbo-
hydrates, 4g total fat
(1g saturated), 1g fiber,
4mg cholesterol,
49mg sodium

Chocolate, vanilla, and zinc (found in yogurt and nuts) may increase sex drive. This is the perfect recipe to share with your sweetheart.

$1/2$ to $3/4$ cup frozen vanilla yogurt

1 tablespoon unsweetened cocoa
    powder

1 to 2 tablespoons hazelnuts

2 to 3 tablespoons milk, to thin

Carrot Cache

Makes 16 ounces.
Per 8-ounce serving:
About 110 calories,
2g protein, 24g carbo-
hydrates, 1g total fat
(trace saturated),
2g fiber, 0mg choles-
terol, 42mg sodium

Of all the orange-colored fruits and vegetables, carrots are the richest in beta carotene. This means that along with helping us with our eyesight (which many of us need about midday after staring at a computer monitor), carrots go a long way in helping to protect our bodies against cancer. Carrots are also good for the heart, circulation, skin, and lungs. An added bonus for men— flaxseed may help suppress the growth of prostate cancer cells.

1 cup carrot-orange juice

3/4 cup frozen diced papaya

1/4 cup beet juice

1 teaspoon ground flaxseed

Pinch freshly grated gingerroot

Heart
Helper I

Makes 16 ounces.
Per 8-ounce serving:
About 149 calories,
5g protein, 13g carbo-
hydrates, 10g total fat
(1g saturated),
5g fiber, 0mg choles-
terol, 21mg sodium

*Heart disease is the number one killer of
men. The Heart Helper smoothies are
filled with heart-friendly ingredients.
The flaxseed (rich in omega-3s) and
avocado in this smoothie will make your
ticker happy.*

$1/2$ Hass avocado, pitted and peeled

$1/2$ frozen banana

1 cup soy milk

1 teaspoon freshly squeezed lime juice

1 teaspoon ground flaxseed

Heart
Helper II

Makes 16 ounces.
Per 8-ounce serving:
About 123 calories,
4g protein, 22g carbo-
hydrates, 3g total fat
(trace saturated),
3g fiber, 0mg choles-
terol, 18mg sodium

*Vitamin B_1, potassium, magnesium,
and lecithin are all good for the heart.
This smoothie has them all.*

1 frozen banana

1 cup soy milk

2 tablespoons pomegranate juice

2 tablespoons pear juice

1 tablespoon wheat germ

1 teaspoon honey

1/2 teaspoon vanilla extract

Heart
Helper III

Bran also helps keep your ticker in good shape.

Makes 16 ounces.

Per 8-ounce serving: About 261 calories, 7g protein, 50g carbohydrates, 5g total fat (2g saturated), 6g fiber, 8mg cholesterol, 57mg sodium

3/4 cup soy milk

1/2 frozen banana

1/2 cup plain yogurt

1/4 cup frozen blueberries

1/4 cup frozen blackberries

2 tablespoons pear juice

1 tablespoon wheat bran

1 tablespoon honey

Mind, Body, and Soul

chapter
5

Hawaii
Five-0

Makes 16 ounces.
Per 8-ounce serving:
About 108 calories,
4g protein, 23g carbo-
hydrates, 2g total fat
(trace saturated),
2g fiber, 0mg choles-
terol, 11mg sodium

This is an all-purpose healing and soothing smoothie. Tofu, rich in protein, is necessary for cell rebuilding and regeneration. Pineapple, an anti-inflammatory, can help soothe a sore throat and is a good source of vitamin C. Lime also has lots of vitamin C and is a powerful antioxidant.

3/4 cup frozen diced pineapple

1/2 cup soy milk

1/2 cup silken tofu

1/2 frozen banana

2 tablespoons guava juice

1 tablespoon freshly squeezed lime juice

Pinch ground cardamom

Soothing
Hibiscus
Wine Cooler

Makes 12 ounces.
Per 12-ounce serving:
About 161 calories,
1g protein, 22g carbo-
hydrates, trace total
fat (trace saturated),
1g fiber, 0mg choles-
terol, 8mg sodium

*Research has shown that moderate
amounts of alcohol may contribute to a
healthy heart. Red wine, in particular,
has antioxidants, which help our bodies
fight disease. In addition to all this
good news, a moderate amount of alcohol is also soothing on the nerves.*

6 frozen cubes strongly brewed
     hibiscus-rose hip tea, or 3/4 cup
     chilled tea
1/2 cup chilled Beaujolais wine or a
     similar light red wine
1/4 cup frozen strawberries
1 tablespoon honey

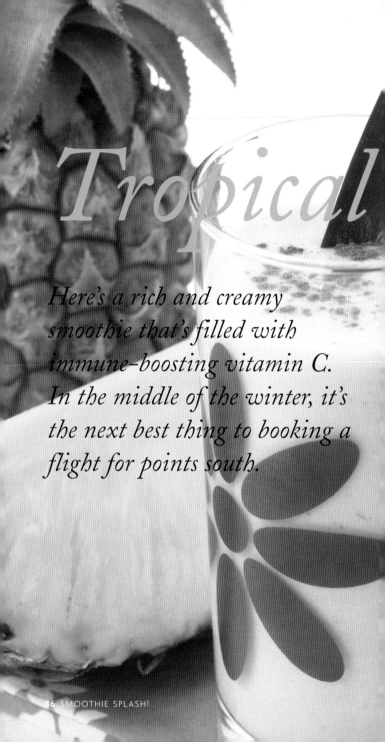

Tropical

Here's a rich and creamy smoothie that's filled with immune-boosting vitamin C. In the middle of the winter, it's the next best thing to booking a flight for points south.

Island Getaway

Makes 16 ounces.
Per 8-ounce serving:
About 152 calories,
1g protein, 21g carbo-
hydrates, 8g total fat
(6g saturated), 2g fiber,
0mg cholesterol,
29mg sodium

1/2 cup diced papaya

1/2 cup frozen diced pineapple

1/2 cup sliced mango

1/2 cup rice milk

1/4 cup unsweetened coconut milk

1/4 teaspoon orange blossom water

Orange Goodness

Makes 16 ounces.
Per 8-ounce serving:
About 66 calories,
4g protein, 8g carbo-
hydrates, 2g total fat
(trace saturated),
3g fiber, 0mg choles-
terol, 18mg sodium

*Orange-colored fruits and vegetables are
rich in beta carotene, an antioxidant
that helps the body fight disease.*

1 cup soy milk

1/2 cup diced papaya

1/4 cup frozen strawberries

2 tablespoons orange-carrot juice

Cornucopia

Makes 16 ounces.
Per 8-ounce serving:
About 139 calories,
4g protein, 25g carbo-
hydrates, 4g total fat
(1g saturated), 4g fiber,
4mg cholesterol,
20mg sodium

*This apricot-laced smoothie is filled
with just about everything you could
want to nourish your whole body, from
your ticker to your bones: antioxidants,
potassium, protein, calcium, manganese,
zinc, riboflavin, and, in the yogurt,
healthy bacteria.*

1/2 cup soy milk

1/2 frozen banana

1/2 cup frozen sliced peaches

1/2 cup frozen blackberries

1/4 cup apricot juice

1/4 cup plain yogurt

1 tablespoon pumpkin seeds

Floral and Fruity

Makes 16 ounces.
Per 8-ounce serving:
About 16 calories,
0g protein, 4g carbo-
hydrates, 0g total fat
(0g saturated),
1g fiber, 0mg choles-
terol, 1mg sodium

The beauty of the deep red color of hibiscus–rose hip tea is surpassed only by its amazing curative powers. Fresh rose hips have the highest proportion of immune–boosting vitamin C of any fruit or vegetable, and when dried the level, though less, is still high. As a matter of fact, barrels of dried rose hips were often given to sailors as part of their rations to prevent scurvy. In addition, tea made from hibiscus flowers has been shown to lower high cholesterol and blood pressure, and it is also a source of vitamin C.

1 1/4 cups chilled strongly brewed
    hibiscus-rose hip tea

1/4 cup frozen strawberries

1/4 cup frozen sliced peaches

Hangover Cure

Makes 16 ounces.
Per 8-ounce serving:
About 185 calories,
5g protein, 40g car-
bohydrates, 1g total
fat (1g saturated),
2g fiber, 4mg choles-
terol, 94mg sodium

Here's a source for many of the nutrients needed to help replace what is lost after a night of drinking and to help counter the aftereffects: fructose, potassium, vitamins C and B, and amino acids. Banana, with its natural antacid, helps with nausea, and milk thistle helps the liver restore itself. Milk thistle has a slight caramel flavor that is boosted by the caramel sauce.

1 frozen banana

1/2 to 3/4 cup frozen vanilla yogurt

1/2 cup frozen strawberries

2 tablespoons caramel sauce

Milk thistle extract, use amount as
    package directs

Liquid vitamin B complex, use amount
    as package directs

2 to 3 tablespoons milk, to thin

Kiwi–Melon Nightcap

Makes 16 ounces.
Per 8-ounce serving:
About 122 calories,
1g protein, 32g carbo-
hydrates, trace total
fat (trace saturated),
2g fiber, 0mg choles-
terol, 10mg sodium

If you have trouble falling asleep at night, try a smoothie nightcap. Among many other medicinal attributes, chamomile tea has mildly sedating and muscle-relaxing effects.

6 frozen cubes strongly brewed
    chamomile tea

8 frozen white grapes

3/4 cup chopped honeydew melon

1 kiwifruit, peeled and chopped

2 teaspoons honey

An Apple

*This smoothie is
rich in boron,
which is reputed
to enhance
memory.*

a Day

Makes 16 ounces.
Per 8-ounce serving:
About 178 calories,
5g protein, 25g carbo-
hydrates, 7g total fat
(2g saturated), 3g fiber,
8mg cholesterol,
54mg sodium

1 chilled apple, peeled, cored, and diced

$1/2$ cup rice milk

$1/2$ cup plain yogurt

1 frozen cube grape juice, or

    2 tablespoons chilled grape juice

1 tablespoon unsweetened unsalted

    peanut butter

1 tablespoon wheat germ

Rosy Cheeks

Makes 16 ounces.
Per 8-ounce serving:
About 210 calories,
5g protein, 16g carbo-
hydrates, 15g total fat
(13g saturated), 1g fiber,
12mg cholesterol,
50mg sodium

A pretty pink smoothie that is high in vitamin A, an important antioxidant that is especially good for our skin and eyes, is just what the dermatologist ordered.

3/4 cup plain yogurt

1/2 cup unsweetened coconut milk

1/2 cup frozen cherries

1/4 cup frozen diced pineapple

2 tablespoons pineapple juice

"B" for Bedtime

Makes 16 ounces.
Per 8-ounce serving:
About 171 calories,
7g protein, 23g carbo-
hydrates, 6g total fat
(3g saturated), 2g fiber,
15mg cholesterol,
80mg sodium

This smoothie is loaded with vitamins B_6 and B_{12}, which have a sedative effect on the nerves and can help you drift off to sleep.

3/4 cup milk

1/2 cup plain yogurt

1/2 cup diced papaya

1/2 frozen banana

1/4 cup carrot-orange juice

1 tablespoon walnuts

1 tablespoon wheat germ

Mind over Matter

Makes 16 ounces.
Per 8-ounce serving:
About 141 calories,
6g protein, 20g carbo-
hydrates, 5g total fat
(2g saturated), 4g fiber,
8mg cholesterol,
39mg sodium

*Nutritional stimulants for the brain—
vitamin B_{12}, manganese, fatty acids,
and tyrosine, a nonessential amino
acid—are abundant here.*

$1/2$ cup frozen sliced peaches

$1/2$ cup frozen blackberries

$1/2$ cup plain yogurt

$1/2$ cup soy milk

1 tablespoon concentrated apple juice

1 tablespoon pumpkin seeds

Nighttime Charley Horse Elixir

Makes 16 ounces.

Per 8-ounce serving:
About 229 calories,
8g protein, 35g carbo-
hydrates, 7g total fat
(3g saturated), 3g fiber,
19mg cholesterol,
91mg sodium

This is a good way to load up on calcium, potassium, and manganese, which together produce a calming effect on the brain and can help induce sleep. Honey, too, has a sedative effect. Potassium and manganese will also help deter leg cramps—the dreaded charley horse—so that you can enjoy a night's sleep without interruption.

1 frozen banana

3/4 cup plain yogurt

3/4 cup milk

1/4 cup frozen sliced peaches

2 tablespoons pear juice

1 tablespoon almond paste

1 tablespoon wheat germ

1 teaspoon honey

Morning Immune Booster

Makes 16 ounces.
Per 8-ounce serving:
About 96 calories,
4g protein, 13g carbo-
hydrates, 4g total fat
(1g saturated),
2g fiber, 0mg choles-
terol, 2mg sodium

When you're feeling a cold coming on,
but you don't feel bad enough to call in
sick, drink this green tea smoothie. It
will give you the jolt of caffeine you need
to get going in the morning and, with
its with antioxidants and vitamin C,
help your body fight infection.

6 frozen cubes strongly brewed green
     tea, or 3/4 cup chilled green tea

3/4 cup soy milk

1/2 cup diced papaya

1/4 cup apricot juice

1 tablespoon pumpkin seeds

1 teaspoon honey

Gingerly Soothing

Ginger will help soothe an upset stomach.

Makes 16 ounces.
Per 8-ounce serving:
About 94 calories,
3g protein, 17g carbo-
hydrates, 2g total fat
(trace saturated),
2g fiber, 0mg choles-
terol, 5mg sodium

1 cup sliced mango

1 cup green tea

$1/2$ cup silken tofu

1 teaspoon freshly grated gingerroot

$1/2$ teaspoon honey

The Purifier

Makes 16 ounces.
Per 8-ounce serving:
About 147 calories,
5g protein, 26g carbo-
hydrates, 3g total fat
(1g saturated), 4g fiber,
4mg cholesterol,
27mg sodium

Blackberries are especially rich in antioxidants and, as a bonus, their crunchy seeds provide valuable fiber.

3/4 cup frozen blackberries

3/4 cup soy milk

1/2 frozen banana

1/4 cup guava juice

1/4 cup plain yogurt

1 tablespoon wheat germ

Tummy Soother

Makes 16 ounces.
Per 8-ounce serving:
About 139 calories,
7g protein, 19g carbo-
hydrates, 5g total fat
(3g saturated),
1g fiber, 18mg choles-
terol, 90mg sodium

Papaya has an active ingredient called papain. It is a digestive aid, and is used to treat ulcers. To augment papain's powers, take a papaya supplement with this delicious smoothie.

1 cup milk

1/2 cup diced papaya

1/2 frozen banana

1/2 cup plain yogurt

Brain Booster

Makes 16 ounces.
Per 8-ounce serving:
About 52 calories, 0g
protein, 14g carbohy-
drates, 0g total fat
(0g saturated),
1g fiber, 0mg choles-
terol, 4mg sodium

The herb ginkgo biloba is said to promote
mental focus. Its flavor is complemented
here by black tea, peach, and ginger.

3 frozen cubes black tea

1 cup chilled black tea

1/2 cup frozen sliced peaches

1 to 2 tablespoons honey

1/8 teaspoon freshly grated gingerroot

Ginkgo biloba extract, use amount
as package directs

Sweet Dreams

Makes 16 ounces.
Per 8-ounce serving:
About 168 calories,
7g protein, 22g carbo-
hydrates, 6g total fat
(3g saturated), 2g fiber,
18mg cholesterol,
90mg sodium

Calcium helps release serotonin, a
neurotransmitter that regulates sleep.
Also, milk contains substances that induce
calm. Calcium is most abundant in dairy
products, but is also in almonds and figs.

1 cup milk

1/2 cup plain yogurt

2 chopped fresh figs, or 2 chopped dried
figs soaked in warm water for 15
minutes to soften

1 tablespoon almond paste

Pinch cardamom

Pineapple Power

Makes 16 ounces.
Per 8-ounce serving:
About 230 calories,
5g protein, 17g carbo-
hydrates, 18g total fat
(14g saturated), 2g fiber,
12mg cholesterol,
52mg sodium

Pineapple contains a powerful enzyme called bromelain, which is useful for reducing muscle and tissue inflammation and as a digestive aid. So if you're suffering from heartburn, sinus congestion, or carpal tunnel syndrome, you've come to the right place.

3/4 cup frozen diced pineapple

3/4 cup plain yogurt

1/2 cup unsweetened coconut milk

2 tablespoons pineapple juice

Morning, Noon, and Night

Fruity Chai

Makes 16 ounces.
Per 8-ounce serving:
About 66 calories,
3g protein, 11g carbo-
hydrates, 2g total fat
(trace saturated),
2g fiber, 0mg choles-
terol, 12mg sodium

*By balancing the spicy flavor of chai—
black tea spiked with cardamom, cinnamon, black pepper, gingerroot, and
cloves—with full-flavored mango and
apricot, this satisfying and nutritious
smoothie is a source of caffeine, protein,
vitamin C, antioxidants, and potassium.*

6 frozen cubes strongly brewed chai,

   or 3/4 cup chilled chai

3/4 cup soy milk

1/2 cup sliced mango

2 tablespoons apricot juice

Chocolate Banana Latte

Makes 16 ounces.
Per 8-ounce serving:
About 100 calories,
3g protein, 19g carbo-
hydrates, 2g total fat
(trace saturated),
2g fiber, 0mg choles-
terol, 53mg sodium

*Enjoy your daily banana and coffee in
the same go. The frozen banana adds
an extra creamy texture and sweetness
to the classic coffee–chocolate combo.*

6 frozen cubes strongly brewed coffee,

   or 3/4 cup chilled coffee

1 cup chocolate soy or dairy milk

1/2 frozen banana

Pinch ground cinnamon, to garnish

Green Tea Plus

Used for 4,000 years as a medicine in China, green tea is now recognized in the West for its many health benefits, including helping with rheumatoid arthritis, high cholesterol levels, cardiovascular disease, infection, and impaired immune levels. Though green tea has less caffeine than coffee—about 60 milligrams per eight-ounce cup compared with 100 milligrams for coffee—it's far and away the healthier caffeinated beverage of choice.

6 frozen cubes strongly brewed green
tea, or 3/4 cup chilled green tea
3/4 cup soy milk
1/2 cup sliced mango
2 tablespoons apricot juice
Pinch cardamom

Frosty

Coffee and chocolate…yum.
Sometimes the only demand
we place on a smoothie is
that it tastes good, and this
icy jolt of caffeine won't
disappoint.

Mocha

Makes 16 ounces.
Per 8-ounce serving:
About 42 calories,
3g protein, 3g carbo-
hydrates, 2g total fat
(trace saturated),
2g fiber, 0mg choles-
terol, 16mg sodium

6 frozen cubes strongly brewed coffee,
   or $3/4$ cup chilled coffee
1 cup chocolate soy or dairy milk
Unsweetened cocoa powder, to garnish
   (optional)

Raisin Bran Delicious

Makes 16 ounces.
Per 8-ounce serving:
About 174 calories,
7g protein, 28g carbo-
hydrates, 5g total fat
(1g saturated), 4g fiber,
4mg cholesterol,
34mg sodium

Sweetened naturally with raisins, this breakfast replacement is as delicious as your favorite bran cereal or muffin, but with the added health benefits of soy and yogurt.

1 frozen banana

1 cup soy milk

1/4 cup silken tofu

1/4 cup plain yogurt

2 tablespoons raisins

1 tablespoon wheat bran

Pinch ground cinnamon

Makes 16 ounces.
Per 8-ounce serving:
About 225 calories,
6g protein, 40g carbo-
hydrates, 6g total fat
(1g saturated), 2g fiber,
0mg cholesterol,
65mg sodium

Prunes have gotten a bad rap over the years—so much so that the California Prune Board lobbied the Food and Drug Administration to officially change the name of its product to dried plums, which they have been called since the new millennium. But the good news is, regardless of their changing image, prunes have always been tasty and filled with lots of cleansing fiber, beta carotene, iron, potassium, and vitamin C.

1/2 cup almond milk

1/2 cup rice milk

1/2 cup silken tofu

1/2 frozen banana

4 dried prunes, soaked in hot water
    for 15 minutes to soften

2 tablespoons apricot juice

2 tablespoons almonds

1 tablespoon wheat germ

1/4 teaspoon vanilla extract

Chai
Sublime

Chai, a spiced black tea, provides a bit of caffeine to add a spring to your step, though not nearly as much as green tea or coffee. Chai and soy milk seem made for each other. Combined with tahini and dates, this naturally rich and sweet treat has protein, calcium, fiber, and iron.

6 frozen cubes strongly brewed chai,
    or 3/4 cup chilled chai

3/4 cup soy milk

4 pitted dates, soaked in water for
    20 minutes to soften

1 tablespoon tahini

Note: If you buy prepared chai, choose the brand with the least sugar added.

Makes **16 ounces.**
Per 8-ounce serving:
About 119 calories,
4g protein, 16g carbo-
hydrates, 5g total fat
(1g saturated), 3g fiber,
0mg cholesterol,
17mg sodium

Mixed Berries and Oats

Makes 16 ounces.
Per 8-ounce serving:
About 143 calories,
3g protein, 31g carbo-
hydrates, 2g total fat
(trace saturated),
4g fiber, 0mg choles-
terol, 60mg sodium

Inspired by a favorite breakfast combination, this yummy smoothie is a quick and easy alternative to making hot oatmeal—and more appealing on a warm day.

1 cup oat milk

1/2 frozen banana

1/4 cup frozen blueberries

1/4 cup frozen strawberries

1/4 cup frozen raspberries

2 tablespoons concentrated apple juice

Beet a Path to Health

Makes 16 ounces.
Per 8-ounce serving:
About 105 calories,
1g protein, 26g carbo-
hydrates, trace total
fat (trace saturated),
1g fiber, 0mg choles-
terol, 45mg sodium

The word on the health circuit these days
is that to be healthy, we need to eat five
servings of fruits and vegetables each
day. With fruits and vegetables in the
same glass, this is a great start.

1 cup sliced mango

1/2 cup apple juice

1/2 cup carrot juice

2 tablespoons beet juice

1/2 teaspoon freshly squeezed lime juice

Pinch freshly grated gingerroot

Hazelnut

Hazelnuts are a nutrient-dense food, especially rich in phosphorous, potassium, copper, zinc, magnesium, selenium, fiber, folic acid, and vitamin E. With this smoothie, you will not only enjoy the distinct flavor of hazelnuts, a classic partner to coffee, but also receive all the nutritional benefits they have to offer.

Coffee
Goodness

6 frozen cubes strongly brewed coffee,
or 3/4 cup chilled coffee

1 cup rice or dairy milk

2 tablespoons hazelnuts

Makes 16 ounces.
Per 8-ounce serving:
About 115 calories,
2g protein, 14g carbo-
hydrates, 6g total fat
(trace saturated),
1g fiber, 0mg choles-
terol, 47mg sodium

Cranberry Pecan

Makes 16 ounces.
Per 8-ounce serving:
About 200 calories,
7g protein, 25g carbo-
hydrates, 9g total fat
(2g saturated), 2g fiber,
8mg cholesterol,
35mg sodium

*Tart, sweet, and chock-full of nutrients—
a great breakfast smoothie.*

$1/2$ cup plain yogurt

$1/2$ cup silken tofu

$1/2$ cup frozen diced pineapple

2 tablespoons orange juice

2 tablespoons cranberry juice

2 tablespoons pecans

1 to 2 tablespoons dried cranberries

1 tablespoon maple syrup

1 tablespoon wheat germ

Banana-Nut Surprise

Makes 16 ounces.
Per 8-ounce serving:
About 212 calories,
8g protein, 28g carbo-
hydrates, 10g total fat
(2g saturated), 5g fiber,
8mg cholesterol,
44mg sodium

Some fruit and nuts—such as bananas and walnuts—make a perfect match. The "surprise" is the cherries, which add a pretty pink color, another level of flavor, and lots of antioxidants.

1 frozen banana

1 cup soy milk

1/2 cup plain yogurt

1/2 cup frozen cherries

2 tablespoons walnuts

1 tablespoon wheat germ

Peaches and Cream

Makes 16 ounces.
Per 8-ounce serving:
About 148 calories,
3g protein, 33g carbo-
hydrates, 2g total fat
(trace saturated),
3g fiber, 0mg choles-
terol, 59mg sodium

Summer and farm-fresh flavors come to mind with this breakfast smoothie. Frozen banana replaces the cream.

1 cup oat milk

3/4 cup frozen sliced peaches

1/2 frozen banana

2 tablespoons concentrated apple juice

Pinch nutmeg

Classic Breakfast Blend

With added protein, this breakfast-in-a-glass should keep you going until lunch. Flaxseed is a good source of fiber, which slows digestion and helps keep you feeling satiated.

Makes 16 ounces.

Per 8-ounce serving: About 133 calories, 6g protein, 22g carbohydrates, 3g total fat (1g saturated), 3g fiber, 4mg cholesterol, 81mg sodium

1 frozen banana

3/4 cup almond milk

1/2 cup frozen strawberries

1/4 cup plain yogurt

2 tablespoons protein powder

1 teaspoon ground flaxseed

Lunch Smoothies:

PBJ

If you enjoy peanut butter and jam between bread, you'll love them in a smoothie. Better yet, if you're a PBJ lover trying to cut down on carbs, you have found nirvana.

Makes 16 ounces.
Per 8-ounce serving:
About 231 calories,
9g protein, 27g carbo-
hydrates, 11g total fat
(3g saturated), 3g fiber,
4mg cholesterol,
29mg sodium

1 frozen banana

$1/2$ cup soy milk

$1/4$ cup plain yogurt

$1/4$ cup silken tofu

2 tablespoons unsweetened, unsalted
        peanut butter

1 tablespoon jam or jelly of choice

Curry in a Hurry

Makes 16 ounces.
Per 8-ounce serving:
About 82 calories,
2g protein, 19g carbo-
hydrates, trace total
fat (0g saturated),
1g fiber, 0mg choles-
terol, 290mg sodium

Inspired by the wonderful flavor of
carrot–orange soup, the rich taste here
is enhanced by vegetable stock, which,
when used as frozen cubes, also adds a
nice thick texture.

4 frozen cubes vegetable stock,
  or 1/2 cup chilled stock

1 cup carrot juice

1/2 cup orange juice

Pinch freshly grated gingerroot

Pinch curry powder

Cool Cucumber

Makes 16 ounces.
Per 8-ounce serving:
About 73 calories,
4g protein, 8g carbo-
hydrates, 3g total fat
(2g saturated), 1g fiber,
12mg cholesterol,
297mg sodium

Cucumbers, sour cream, and dill are a classic combination. Substituting yogurt for sour cream, this light smoothie evokes the crisp flavor of fresh cukes and dill picked from a garden.

4 frozen cubes vegetable stock,
     or 1/2 cup chilled stock
3/4 cup peeled, seeded, and chopped
     cucumber
3/4 cup plain yogurt
1/4 cup chopped scallions
1 tablespoon freshly squeezed
     lemon juice
1/8 teaspoon snipped fresh dill
Pinch salt

Creamy Gazpacho

Avocado adds a rich and creamy texture to savory vegetables and yogurt. Nutritious, and easy to prepare, it's a great midday refresher or accompaniment to lunch or dinner.

Makes 16 ounces.
Per 8-ounce serving:
About 91 calories, 2g protein, 10g carbohydrates, 5g total fat (1g saturated), 2g fiber, 4mg cholesterol, 331mg sodium

1 cup vegetable juice

1/4 Hass avocado

1/4 cup chopped red bell pepper

1/4 cup plain yogurt

2 teaspoons lime juice

2 to 3 drops red or green hot pepper sauce, or to taste

Minty Fresh

At once savory and sweet, this subtle, minty-fresh smoothie has a high water content, making it the perfect cooldown on a hot day. Frozen grapes add a nice thickness and chill.

Makes 16 ounces.
Per 8-ounce serving:
About 73 calories,
3g protein, 12g carbo-
hydrates, 2g total fat
(1g saturated), 1g fiber,
8mg cholesterol,
34mg sodium

3/4 cup chopped honeydew melon

8 frozen white grapes

1/2 cup cucumber, peeled, seeded,
and chopped

1/2 cup plain yogurt

2 or 3 mint leaves

Pinch salt

Garden Fresh

Brimming with vegetable flavor, here's a garden-fresh treat that will keep your savory taste buds happy.

Makes 16 ounces.
Per 8-ounce serving:
About 34 calories,
1g protein, 8g carbo-
hydrates, 0g total fat,
1g fiber, 0mg choles-
terol, 313mg sodium

1 cup mixed vegetable juice

1/4 cup seeded, chopped sweet
red pepper

1/4 cup peeled, seeded, and chopped
cucumber

1/4 cup chopped scallions

1/8 teaspoon snipped fresh dill

1 to 2 drops hot pepper sauce

Pinch salt

Summer Sweet Tea

Makes 16 ounces.
Per 8-ounce serving:
About 92 calories,
3g protein, 18g carbo-
hydrates, 2g total fat
(trace saturated),
3g fiber, 0mg choles-
terol, 12mg sodium

*Sweetened with honey and guava juice,
this summery and refreshing peach-berry
combination will satisfy green tea lovers
with a bit of a sweet tooth.*

6 frozen cubes strongly brewed green
    tea, or 3/4 cup chilled green tea

3/4 cup soy milk

1/4 cup frozen sliced peaches

1/4 cup frozen blackberries

1/4 cup guava juice

2 teaspoons honey

Dessert Smoothies:

Tropical

Balancing the fresh flavor of pineapple with the creaminess of frozen yogurt and the mild yet distinctive flavor of pistachios, this smoothie will satisfy your craving for something sweet, but not too rich.

Sweet Tooth

Makes 12 ounces.
Per 12-ounce serving:
About 352 calories,
7g protein, 39g carbo-
hydrates, 21g total fat
(15g saturated),
3g fiber, 10mg choles-
terol, 111mg sodium

$1/2$ to $3/4$ cup vanilla frozen yogurt
or vanilla ice cream

$1/2$ cup frozen diced pineapple

$1/4$ cup unsweetened coconut milk

1 to 2 tablespoons pistachios

Russian Revolution

Makes 16 ounces.
Per 8-ounce serving:
About 140 calories,
4g protein, 30g carbo-
hydrates, 1g total fat
(trace saturated),
0g fiber, 4mg choles-
terol, 373mg sodium

It's worth the effort to make fresh beet juice for this vegetarian twist on borscht. The color of beet juice is simply gorgeous, and the taste is delicious and surprisingly sweet—or perhaps not so surprisingly, since beets have the highest sugar content of all vegetables.

4 frozen cubes vegetable stock,
    or $1/2$ cup chilled stock

1 cup beet juice

$1/4$ cup carrot juice

$1/4$ cup plain yogurt

1 tablespoon apple juice

1 teaspoon freshly squeezed lemon juice

$1/8$ teaspoon snipped fresh dill

Pinch chopped garlic

Pinch salt

Pinch pepper

Almond Joy

Makes 12 ounces.
Per 12-ounce serving:
About 427 calories,
8g protein, 55g carbo-
hydrates, 22g total fat
(15g saturated fat),
4g fiber, 10mg choles-
terol, 126mg sodium

Banana adds a twist to the retro flavor combination of chocolate and almonds—a treat inspired by a famous candy bar brand that has endured for more than 50 years.

1/2 to 3/4 cup vanilla frozen yogurt
    or ice cream

1/2 frozen banana

1/4 cup unsweetened coconut milk

1 to 2 tablespoons almonds

1 tablespoon chocolate syrup

Nutty Black Forest

Makes 12 ounces.
Per 12-ounce serving:
About 239 calories,
6g protein, 35g carbo-
hydrates, 10g total fat
(3g saturated),
3g fiber, 11mg choles-
terol, 104mg sodium

The rich flavor and crunchy texture of macadamia nuts enhances the delicious chocolate-and-cherry combination inspired by Black Forest cake.

1/2 to 3/4 cup chocolate frozen yogurt
   or ice cream*

1/4 cup frozen cherries

1 to 2 tablespoons macadamia nuts

2 to 3 tablespoons chocolate milk,
   to thin

Substitution: Use vanilla frozen yogurt
or ice cream and regular milk with 2
tablespoons chocolate syrup.

Ambrosia

Makes 12 ounces.

Per 12-ounce serving:
About 347 calories,
6g protein, 40g carbo-
hydrates, 20g total fat
(15g saturated), 3g fiber,
27mg cholesterol,
58mg sodium

Fruity, light, and creamy, with that certain je ne sais quoi of orange-blossom water, here is a drink that truly is the food of the gods.

1/2 to 3/4 cup vanilla ice cream or
    frozen yogurt

1/2 frozen banana

1/4 cup frozen diced pineapple

3 tablespoons orange juice

2 tablespoons unsweetened flaked coconut

2 tablespoons unsweetened coconut milk

1/2 teaspoon orange-blossom water

2 to 3 tablespoons milk, to thin

German Chocolate Cake

Makes 12 ounces.
Per 12-ounce serving:
About 265 calories,
6g protein, 32g carbo-
hydrates, 15g total fat
(8g saturated), 3g fiber,
11mg cholesterol,
107mg sodium

Some classic combinations are as good sipped from a tall, cold glass as they are served on a plate with a fork. This is one of them.

1/2 to 3/4 cup chocolate frozen yogurt
or ice cream*

2 tablespoons unsweetened flaked
coconut

1 to 2 tablespoons pecans

2 to 3 tablespoons chocolate milk,
to thin

Substitution: Use vanilla frozen yogurt
or ice cream and regular milk with 2
tablespoons chocolate syrup.

Cocktails

Berry Refreshing

Makes 12 ounces.
Per 12-ounce serving:
About 159 calories,
0g protein, 8g carbo-
hydrates, trace total
fat (0g saturated),
1g fiber, 0mg choles-
terol, 1mg sodium

As with all smoothies in this book, freezing fresh, ripe fruit yourself produces the best results. Here, the refreshing flavor of frozen strawberries, sweetened just a touch, takes center stage.

1/4 cup frozen strawberries

2 ounces vodka

1/2 ounce freshly squeezed lime juice

1 teaspoon simple syrup (recipe below)

1/2 cup crushed ice

Garnish: Coat the rim of a martini glass with granulated sugar before pouring the smoothie (optional)

Simple Syrup

1 cup water

2 cups sugar

Combine the sugar and the water in a small saucepan. Heat to a boil while stirring. Reduce heat and continue to stir until the sugar dissolves, about 3 minutes. Let cool to room temperature. Using a funnel, pour simple syrup into a container that will hold at least a cup and a half. The syrup should keep indefinitely in the refrigerator, though on rare occasion it may ferment and sour. To be safe, make sure to test simple syrup that's more than a month old before using in cocktails.

Between the Sheets

Makes 12 ounces.
Per 12-ounce serving:
About 294 calories,
0g protein, 8g carbo-
hydrates, 0g total fat
(0g saturated), 0g
fiber, 0mg choles-
terol, 3mg sodium

This drink, which has not only an adult name but also a wonderfully adult taste, is for smoothie makers who unabashedly enjoy the taste of alcohol. The touch of sour lemon is perfectly matched with the sweeter natures of brandy, rum, and Cointreau, creating a smooth drink in which everything hangs in the balance— or, between the sheets.

2 ounces brandy

1 ounce light rum

1 ounce Cointreau liqueur or other
    triple sec liqueur

1/2 ounce freshly squeezed lemon juice

1 cup crushed ice

Piña

With the addition of frozen pineapple, this famous tropical drink—destined to be enjoyed in a lounge chair alongside a pool or crashing waves—is even more delicious.

Colada

1/4 cup frozen diced pineapple

1 ounce light or gold rum

1 ounce pineapple juice

1 ounce cream of coconut

1/2 cup crushed ice

Makes 12 ounces.
Per 12-ounce serving:
About 131 calories,
1g protein, 13g carbo-
hydrates, 1g total fat
(1g saturated), 1g fiber,
3mg cholesterol,
48mg sodium

Fallen Leaves

Makes 12 ounces.

Per 12-ounce serving:
About 266 calories,
0g protein, 12g carbo-
hydrates, trace total
fat (0g saturated),
0g fiber, 0mg choles-
terol, 7mg sodium

Like its name, this drink's earthy apple flavor conjures up the turn of seasons when we savor the crisp scent of autumn in the air. A richly textured drink, its flavor is best savored next to a crackling fire, but really, anywhere will do.

2 ounces Calvados or other apple brandy

1 ounce brandy

$1/2$ ounce sweet vermouth

$1/2$ ounce dry vermouth

1 ounce concentrated apple juice

Pinch grated lemon zest

1 cup crushed ice

Note: You may substitute any apple brandy for Calvados. However, since Calvados tends to be the driest of the apple brandies, you should use less con-centrated apple juice if you substitute.

Island Express

Makes 12 ounces.
Per 12-ounce serving:
About 83 calories,
0g protein, 5g carbo-
hydrates, 0g total fat,
0g fiber, 0mg choles-
terol, 3mg sodium

With only one ounce of rum, this light cranberry-citrus drink is refreshing any-time, but especially on a hot summer day.

1 ounce white rum

$1/2$ ounce freshly squeezed lime juice

$1/2$ ounce cranberry juice

$1/2$ ounce orange juice

1 cup crushed ice

New Zealander

Makes 12 ounces.
Per 12-ounce serving:
About 229 calories,
1g protein, 25g carbo-
hydrates, 1g total fat
(trace saturated),
5g fiber, 0mg choles-
terol, 7mg sodium

Kiwifruit is the star here, contributing an agreeably tart and distinctive flavor and a delicate, pale green color.

1 kiwifruit, peeled and chopped

2 ounces vodka

$1/2$ ounce freshly squeezed lime juice

$1/2$ ounce simple syrup (page 136)

$1/2$ cup crushed ice

Pomegranate Margarita

Pomegranate juice lends great flavor and a beautiful tinge of crimson to the margarita—the classic tequila lover's drink.

Makes 12 ounces.
Per 12-ounce serving:
About 264 calories,
0g protein, 47g carbo-
hydrates, 0g total fat,
0g fiber, 0mg choles-
terol, 10mg sodium

2 ounces white tequila

1/2 ounce Cointreau liqueur

1/2 ounce orange juice

1/2 ounce freshly squeezed lime juice

1/2 ounce pomegranate juice

1 cup crushed ice

Twist of lime, to garnish

Chocolate Martini

Makes 12 ounces.
Per 12-ounce serving:
About 163 calories, 0g
protein, 4g carbohy-
drates, 0g total fat
(0g saturated), 0g
fiber, 0mg choles-
terol, 1mg sodium

Ahhh, the chocolate martini—a delicious result of the many "anything goes" martinis invented during the last decade of the previous century.

2 ounces vodka

1/2 ounce Godiva liqueur

1 cup ice

Garnish: Dust the rim of the martini glass with unsweetened cocoa powder before pouring in the drink.

Variation: To enjoy as an after-dinner drink, use equal portions of vodka and Godiva liqueur.

Up and Down

Makes 12 ounces.
Per 12-ounce serving:
About 151 calories,
0g protein, 17g carbo-
hydrates, trace total
fat (0g saturated),
0g fiber, 0mg choles-
terol, 5mg sodium

2 ounces vodka

1/2 ounce Kahlúa liqueur

2 frozen cubes strongly brewed coffee,
or 1/4 cup chilled coffee

1/2 cup ice

Note: If you use chilled coffee instead of frozen cubes, increase ice to 1 cup for thick consistency.

Fuzzy Navel

A fresh-tasting twist on a popular drink substitutes frozen peach slices for peach schnapps.

Makes 12 ounces.
Per 12-ounce serving:
About 152 calories,
1g protein, 14g carbo-
hydrates, trace total
fat (0g saturated),
2g fiber, 0mg choles-
terol, 1mg sodium

1/2 cup frozen sliced peaches

1 1/2 ounces orange juice

1 ounce vodka

1/4 cup ice

Bourbon Ball

Makes 12 ounces.
Per 12-ounce serving:
About 214 calories,
2g protein, 5g carbo-
hydrates, 6g total fat
(1g saturated), 2g fiber,
2mg cholesterol,
5mg sodium

Based on the flavor combination of the traditional holiday sweet, a Bourbon Ball smoothie doubles as after-dinner drink and dessert in one.

$1/2$ to $3/4$ cup vanilla ice cream

2 ounces bourbon

1 to 2 tablespoons pecans

1 tablespoon unsweetened cocoa powder

Garnish: Dust the rim of the martini glass with additional cocoa powder before pouring the smoothie.

Off the Vine

Makes 12 ounces.
Per 12-ounce serving:
About 168 calories,
0g protein, 10g carbo-
hydrates, trace total
fat (0g saturated), 0g
fiber, 0mg choles-
terol, 2mg sodium

Cîroc, a French vodka distilled from grapes, is an exciting new flavor that makes a delicious drink when combined with frozen white grapes and guava juice.

2 ounces Cîroc vodka

6 frozen white grapes

1 ounce guava juice

$1/2$ cup ice

Brandy Alexander

Makes 12 ounces.
Per 12-ounce serving:
About 352 calories,
1g protein, 32g carbo-
hydrates, 4g total fat
(3g saturated), 0g fiber,
16mg cholesterol,
30mg sodium

Made originally with cream, the Brandy Alexander has been around since Prohibition. It's thought that the cream was added to disguise the rough swill then available at speakeasies. Regardless, it's a delicious drink that's survived to this day for good reason.

1/2 to 3/4 cup vanilla ice cream

2 ounces brandy

1 1/2 ounces dark crème de cacao

Freshly grated nutmeg, to garnish

Variation: Add 1/2 frozen banana (and use less ice cream)

Brandy Blast

If a drink with the name "Orgasm" didn't already exist, this divine Nutella–brandy creation would have been called something else. Enough said.

2 ounces brandy

2 tablespoons Nutella spread

1/2 to 3/4 cup vanilla ice cream

Note: Mix brandy and Nutella in blender before adding ice cream.

Makes 12 ounces.
Per 12-ounce serving:
About 457 calories, 5g protein, 37g carbohydrates, 18g total fat (7g saturated), 2g fiber, 30mg cholesterol, 70mg sodium

Strawberry Daiquiri

Makes 12 ounces.
Per 12-ounce serving:
About 190 calories,
1g protein, 14g carbo-
hydrates, trace total
fat (0g saturated),
2g fiber, 0mg choles-
terol, 1mg sodium

The classic daiquiri of rum, lime, and simple syrup has been nearly forgotten, and now the strawberry daiquiri reigns supreme. It's an exquisite drink, perfect for the summertime harvest of berries. Why not sip it as the coals heat up in the barbecue?

1/2 cup frozen strawberries

1 1/2 ounces light rum

3/4 ounce freshly squeezed lime juice

1/2 ounce Cointreau liqueur

1 teaspoon simple syrup (page 136)

1/2 cup ice

Classic Margarita

Makes 12 ounces.
Per 12-ounce serving:
About 316 calories,
0g protein, 12g carbo-
hydrates, 0g total fat,
0g fiber, 0mg choles-
terol, 1mg sodium

The frozen margarita has been around for a while, so its entrance into smoothie kingdom is no big surprise. Whip one up to enjoy on its own, or with some chips and salsa.

2 1/2 ounces white tequila

1 1/2 ounces Cointreau liqueur

3/4 ounce freshly squeezed lime juice

1 cup ice

Garnish: Coat the rim of the glass with salt before pouring in the margarita (optional).

Yuletide Joy

A holiday favorite that puts you in the spirit and also satisfies your sweet tooth.

Makes 12 ounces.

Per 12-ounce serving:
About 357 calories,
3g protein, 15g carbo-
hydrates, 10g total fat
(5g saturated), 0g fiber,
25mg cholesterol,
96mg sodium

$1/2$ to $3/4$ cup eggnog ice cream,
     or 4 to 6 cubes frozen eggnog

1 ounce bourbon

1 ounce brandy

1 ounce dark rum

Freshly grated nutmeg, to garnish

Hibiscus
Breeze

Makes 12 ounces.
Per 12-ounce serving:
About 171 calories,
0g protein, 11g carbo-
hydrates, 0g total fat,
1g fiber, 0mg choles-
terol, 1mg sodium

*A surprising combination of beautifully
colored, soothing tea with pineapple
and peach flavors, this is the perfect
drink to help you wind down after a
long day.*

$1/4$ cup frozen sliced peaches

2 ounces vodka

1 $1/2$ ounces pineapple juice

$1/2$ ounce chilled hibiscus–rose hip tea

$1/2$ cup ice

Index

M

N

O

P

Q

R